£14·99

D0754433

Glanmor Williams: A Life

GLANMOR WILLIAMS

❧

A Life

UNIVERSITY OF WALES PRESS
CARDIFF
2002

© Glanmor Williams, 2002

First published 2002
Reprinted 2002

British Library Cataloguing-in-Publication Data.
A catalogue record for this book is available from the British Library.

ISBN 0–7083–1745–6

All rights reserved. No part of this book may be reproduced, stored in a retrieval system, or transmitted, in any form or by any means, electronic, mechanical, photocopying, recording or otherwise, without clearance from the University of Wales Press, 10 Columbus Walk, Brigantine Place, Cardiff CF10 4UP.
www.wales.ac.uk/press

First edition published with the financial assistance of the W. T. Mainwaring-Hughes Memorial Fund, University of Wales Swansea.

The right of Glanmor Williams to be identified as author of this work has been asserted by him in accordance with the Copyright, Designs and Patents Act 1988.

Typeset at University of Wales Press
Printed in Great Britain by Dinefwr Press, Llandybïe

Contents

Preface   vii

I	Bachgen bach o Ddowlais	1
II	Early schooldays	16
III	Life in 'the Castle'	29
IV	'The College by the Sea', 1937–1942	42
V	The 'County School'	62
VI	Academic apprenticeship	74
VII	The groves of Academe	87
VIII	Disturbed waters	104
IX	Calls from many quarters	118
X	The broadcasting arena	132
XI	The world of books and information	149
XII	Academic run-down	162
XIII	Clearing up the backlog	177
XIV	Retrospect	195

Index   200

List of illustrations

Glanmor Williams aged three   2
G.W. aged four with his father and mother   8
Grandfather James Evans   24
G.W. in Cyfarthfa Castle Grammar School aged twelve   31
Committee of the Celtic Society, Aberystwyth, 1941   51
G.W. as president of the Students' Representative Council,
    1941–2   57
Joint Students' Representative Council, UCW and UCL,
    1941–2   58
Wedding photograph, April 1946   81
The family, 1965   101
1962 portrait   108
The Department of History, Swansea, 1964   113
G.W. with Mrs P. M. ('Ginge') Thomas   115
With Princess Margaret at the opening of the BBC
    headquarters, 1967   133
The Broadcasting Council for Wales, June 1971   146
G.W, with Professor Gareth Elwyn Jones, 1990   178
Bidding farewell to Cadw, 1994, with Sir Wyn Roberts   185
The Chairmen and Secretaries of the Royal
    Commissions on Ancient Monuments, England, Wales
    and Scotland, 1989   186
Investiture at Buckingham Palace, 1996   193

Preface

I did not originally plan to write an autobiography. It all sprang from a lecture on my recollections of the early years I spent in my home town of Dowlais, which Dr Joseph Gross and Dr T. F. Holley persuaded me to deliver. That talk was well enough received for it subsequently to be published in the *Merthyr Historian* VI (1993), and led to my being invited to publish the second, third, fourth and fifth instalments in the *Merthyr Historian* VII (1994), VIII (1996), IX (1998) and X (1999). At this point, I had reached the end of the story of the time I had spent in the Merthyr district.

It now dawned on me that, whether or not I had intended to do so at the outset, I had in fact written an account of about a quarter of my life's history. This realization prompted me to think seriously of the possibility of completing my recollections. Having done so, I sent the finished manuscript to the University of Wales Press, whose director, Ms Susan Jenkins, was, as always, distinctly encouraging in her attitude. I am deeply grateful to her and her colleagues, Ms Ceinwen Jones and Ms Liz Powell, for all they have done in ensuring that the volume appeared in print. I should also like to express my gratitude to the W. T. Mainwaring-Hughes Memorial Fund for its generous assistance, the anonymous Press reader for helpful comments, Mrs Gloria Watkins for typing so much of the manuscript for me, Professor Ralph A. Griffiths for his help and advice and Dr Richard Welchman for his unfailingly cheerful support. My thanks are due, too, to Dr Gross and Dr Holley for their interest and friendship over many years, as well as for unwittingly acting as 'midwives' for the book. What I owe my wife is beyond praise.

March 2002

I

Bachgen bach o Ddowlais

Bachgen bach o Ddowlais
Yn eistedd ar bwys y tân.

(A little boy from Dowlais sitting by the fire.)

or, as Dowlais people would certainly have said in days gone by

Bachan bêch o Ddowlish
Yn ishta ar bwys y tên.

'Bachan bêch o Ddowlish': that is what I have always been and very largely what I still am. I look back on the people of my native heath with the deepest pride and affection. The Dowlais of my youth was a typical south Wales industrial community whose inhabitants were in the main ordinary working people with no pretensions to money or position. I remember them as wonderful folk, true members of the industrial *gwerin*: hard-working, warm-hearted, kindly and hospitable, willing to share their last crust with others and marvellously brave and supportive of one another in adversity. They had a real sense of shared values; they were, and are, to me the salt of the earth. The older I get the more I admire them and the more sorely I regret the passing of that kind of community. I do not think that this is just sentimental *hiraeth* or nostalgia on my part. My own impressions were vividly confirmed some years ago by Dr Roderick Bowen, at one time MP for Cardiganshire. He told me

Glanmor Williams aged three.

how, in the 1920s, his brother had come to live and work in Dowlais and was loud in his praise of the kindness and warmth of Dowlais people. Dr Bowen went on to say how greatly he enjoyed visiting his brother and how much he envied his living amid the outgoing generosity of such attractive people.

Looking back on what life was like in the Dowlais of the 1920s and 1930s I am struck by the extraordinary paradoxes that characterized it then. At the time, of course, those contradictions did not strike me at all. Like most other youngsters I just enjoyed life and lived it unthinkingly. The existence I knew was the only one I had experienced; I took it all as part of the natural order of things. Indeed, I suppose I assumed that most people lived a similar sort of life. But with the passing of the years those paradoxes have come to stand out more plainly; and there are five of them which particularly strike me.

First, Dowlais was old as an industrial community. It had been in existence for 150 years even in the 1920s; and yet it was sited on the very borderline between the crowded industrial communities of Glamorgan and the rural peace and beauty of southern Breconshire. Secondly, it had for a century and a half been an extraordinarily successful and prosperous hive of industry, and yet within a few years it was devastated by an economic depression of quite unprecedented intensity. Thirdly, it was a community peopled for the most part by Welsh men and women who had flocked in from Welsh-speaking rural communities in earlier generations. These incomers had naturally brought their native language and their social attitudes with them. By the 1920s, however, Dowlais had become an essentially English-speaking community, especially among those under thirty years of age. Fourthly, those Welsh immigrants had also brought their religious and spiritual ideals with them and had created a series of large, powerful Welsh chapels which more or less dominated the social and cultural affiliations of the town as well as its religious life. Nevertheless, side by side with the Nonconformity there also flourished a strong worldly and non-religious, if not irreligious, disposition. Finally, Merthyr and Dowlais had had the reputation since the 1860s, and perhaps as far back as 1831 (the year of the great Merthyr Riot), of being one of the major strongholds of radical and liberal political activity. After the Great War of 1914–18 its earlier liberalism was rapidly being superseded by the growth of socialist loyalties.

Dowlais, as one of the earliest industrial communities of Wales, had been founded on the basis of iron and coal. It was virtually the creation of a single family – the Guests. That notable strain had left its mark everywhere in the town: in the great ironworks; the endless lines of trucks bearing the sacred initials GKN; even the names of the streets – Guest Cottages, Ivor Street, Charlotte Street, and so on – and those of many individuals – Ivor, Charlotte, Josiah – commemorated them. The unmistakable stamp of the family could also be seen on all the biggest and grandest buildings in the town: Dowlais House, parish churches, the Guest Memorial Library, Dowlais School and the Dowlais Stables, which provided better accommodation for horses than human beings, and which Dr Joseph Gross, that champion of Merthyr's history, worked so hard to save some years ago. All were monumentally built on classical lines with massive dressed stone. The one that I remember with most affection disappeared many years ago – Dowlais Market. How vividly I remember my attendance on Saturday mornings, hypnotized by the entrancing smells, particularly of fresh faggots and green peas, and listening spellbound to the mesmerizing eloquence of the travelling salesmen! I was so convinced by the persuasive sales talk of one pedlar of patent medicines that, at the age of eight, I went home and tremblingly confessed to my mother that I thought I was in the terminal throes of prostate gland trouble.

When the huge furnaces were working, the lurid glare from them turned night into day in a sort of pseudo-sunset that lit up the sky and could be seen for miles around. Another unforgettable sight was that of the hundreds of colliers returning from the Rhymney Valley pits and debouching from Caeharris Station. They then marched down the High Street in their working clothes, with their hands and faces black with coal dust. There was no talk of pithead baths in those days! Tramping down the road in their heavy hobnailed boots, the reverberations of which left the air resounding with their noise, they looked rather like native regiments from the depths of Africa. It was a familiar sight for us, but I remember a friend who, before 1914, used to come to Dowlais as a packman from Newcastle Emlyn telling me that, when he had first seen this fearsome sight of hordes of black-faced men, he had been frightened out of his wits.

But, though this was unmistakably an industrial township, it stood only a mile or two from the Breconshire county boundary. Even as children making our way to Pant School we used to have to walk past the fields of farms with such evocative old Welsh names as Hafod, Cwmrhydybedd and Caerhaca (this last-named corrupted by us to 'Cracker'). We were accustomed to seeing livestock grazing in the fields and were familiar with the changing seasons and tasks of the agricultural year. We were as used to playing out on the commons of the Brynna (Bryniau) or the Twynau as on the streets of the town. One of our keenest delights as children was to go on picnics to the unspoiled villages of Pont-sarn or Vaynor or Pontsticill, or even to venture a little further afield to Torpantau, Tal-y-bont or Penderyn. When, along with a number of my friends, I acquired a bike in my early teens, we felt that this had given us quite exceptional freedom to explore at leisure the valleys of the Taf Fawr and the Taf Fechan. We especially loved to roam among their reservoirs which, though man-made, were as delectable as any natural lakes. Occasionally, we went on 'tea parties' to neighbouring Monmouthshire, especially to the Gilwern area. Many will know that Gilwern's supreme attraction was the boating it offered on the canal there. One episode remains indelibly etched on my memory. The senior deacon of our chapel was a patriarchal figure who ranked somewhere just below Moses or Elijah on my boyish scale of values. There he stood on the canalside at Gilwern, one foot on the bank, the other in a boat. Gradually, his craft began to glide from the shore, leaving him in more and more of a quandary, not knowing which foot to raise. His agony was not prolonged, but while it lasted it created consternation in our youthful minds. Could it possibly be part of the divine purpose that so august and consecrated a personage was going to fall into the canal? If, horror of horrors, he did, would it be permissible for us to follow our instincts and laugh uproariously? When eventually he plunged into the cold depths

I am afraid I have to admit that our awareness of the ridiculous got the better of our sense of the sacred.

Dowlais had for most of its history been a flourishing place. Its iron industry, kept at the technological forefront by a succession of remarkably gifted industrialists and managers, had been so successful that it had drawn in thousands of people. Perhaps it should be emphasized that they had been attracted to Dowlais from the countryside, not compelled to come. In spite of the not infrequent slumps, the periodic unemployment and short-time working, the heavy incidence of accidents at work, the over-crowded dwellings, the regular outbreaks of disease and the other misfortunes we associate with industrial conditions, people had come because of the prospect of earning much higher wages than any available to them in the rural localities and because of the many attractions of living in a town. They had done very well before 1914 and they expected 'normal' condi-tions to return after 1918. But the good times never really came back. The difficulties of the immediate post-war era were followed by the strike of 1926 and the appalling depression which set in during the late 1920s. The ironworks were virtually closed down, and many of the miners were either unemployed or on short time. Unemployment and poverty were rife, with a great cloud of sadness and despair closing in on the town. Many of the shops along the once-busy streets were forced to close and remained closed; they always gave the impression of staring hopelessly through blank and sightless windows. It used to be reckoned that Dowlais and Jarrow shared the unenviable distinction of being the two places in the UK hardest hit by the depression.

It took some time for people to realize that the slump was going to last so long, but gradually, as the realization dawned, those who could began to emigrate in increasing numbers from the town to find work. It was not only the young and single who left; whole families pulled up their tent pegs and departed. Those who were left found the going desperately hard. Many of them were proud and intelligent individuals who found the prospect of being dumped on the social scrap-heap intolerable. People became thinner and more haggard with every year that passed, their clothes shabbier and more ill-fitting, the threadbare mufflers no longer able to conceal how gaunt and scrawny their necks had become. I still carry in my mind the image of one among many, the lineaments of whose sad face had so impressed a documentary film-maker that he used it as his opening shot. He was a man in his fifties who had once had a responsible job but had been unemployed for years. He had a very typical Welsh appearance: a thatch of wiry black hair long gone white, a bold aquiline nose now looking unusually bony, long deeply incised lines along his sunken cheeks, and, worst of all, deep-set eyes, which seemed so large and questioning and dogged with despair. I remember, too, when I went first to the secondary school, seeing some of my schoolmates throw themselves on the school dinners with what seemed to me to be, even by the standards of hungry schoolboys, barbaric gluttony, until I quickly came to realize that this was the only decent meal they could hope for in the course of the day.

Yet, in face of all this hardship caused by the depression, the spirit of the people, though damped, was certainly never extinguished. Looking back to all the poverty and the inexorable pressure it put on old and young, it is impossible not to admire the courage shown in those days: the willingness of hard-pressed parents to sacrifice on behalf of their children; the unceasing efforts to make ends meet; the painful struggles to keep youngsters in school as long as possible so that they might perhaps have a better chance than an earlier generation. Yet, strikingly enough, there was no mention of the child abuse so sadly prevalent in our own generation. How much of it existed beneath the surface, I cannot tell; what I can certainly say is that I never saw any sign of it even among the poorest families. What stood out most plainly was the never-ending courage and tenacity of the wives and mothers. They were the most shining heroes of the whole community, though their praises were rarely if ever sung. Perhaps it was all summed up in the reactions of Edward, Prince of Wales, when he visited the town in 1936. He was reliably reported to have said in the almost unbelieving tones of one who had been shell-shocked by what he saw: 'Oh! such nightmarish hardship! God help them. Something *must* be

G.W. aged four with his father and mother.

done.' Possibly the prince left it to God to do his part, but nothing much seems to have resulted from what he said. Lloyd George was another who made a memorable comment. In a speech at the National Eisteddfod he recalled a well-known Welsh lyric poem to the nightingale in which the poet marvelled at the way in which the bird was able to go on singing despite the pain caused by a thorn beneath its breast. Lloyd George likened the people of the industrial valleys of south Wales to that nightingale – singing in spite of the agony caused by the depression. It was a striking comparison, though it, again, did little to lighten the load.

The neighbourhood was overwhelmingly Welsh in spirit and outlook. As in other similar communities the range of names was inclined to be restricted. Most of us tended to be Williamses, Evanses, Davieses, Joneses, Thomases and so on. Nor was the span of Christian names all that much wider: there were many David Johns or William Thomases or Mary Anns and Sarah

Janes. It was rarely that an exotic plant like 'Glanmor' blossomed in their midst. So nicknames perforce flourished like the buds in May. Some were known by the jobs they did – *barbwr* (barber) or *halier* (haulier) and one whole family was dubbed the 'donkeys' – not because they were more than ordinarily dull or stubborn, but because one of their ancestors had been in charge of a donkey engine. Others were known by the place where they lived – Bili Ben-pwll, Gwen Pwllyrhwyaid and a whole clan known as the 'Ships', not on account of any nautical proclivities on their part but because they lived in a public house called The Ship. Sometimes that mischievous sense of humour combined with social criticism, so greatly treasured by the local people, surfaced in names like the *talu forys* (pay tomorrows) or the *mesur prins* (short measures). But the names which tickled me most were the double-barrelled 'Ifan Difarws' (Ifan Repented) for the husband, and 'Jane Gâs Lwc' (Jane Got Lucky) for the wife. My father's eldest sister, my Aunt Mary, who had an encyclopaedic knowledge of these and other matters concerning the locality, explained to me that as a young man Ifan had been courting an extremely pretty girl who had, alas, jilted him. Bitterly cast down by this untoward rejection, he almost immediately married the very plain Jane on the rebound, and lived to regret the bargain, while she made the most of her unexpected luck.

A few outlying parts of the district, like Caeharris at the top end of Dowlais, or Heolgerrig on the mountainside at the west end of Merthyr, remained pretty strongly Welsh in speech. But it has to be admitted that most of the area had become largely Anglicized by the 1920s. That was probably due to two main factors: firstly, the huge influx of non-Welsh-speakers and, secondly, the nature of the school system, which virtually ignored the Welsh language. Among the non-Welsh speakers, in addition to the many who had come from various parts of England, there was a large body of Irish people, against whom there was always a good deal of prejudice. The Irish tended to live in the poorest and most overcrowded quarters and they were all Roman Catholics. As a result, they were known to us as 'Plant Mari' (Mary's children) and their Catholic priest was disparagingly referred to as 'y pab' (the pope). Another sizeable element consisted of Spaniards. The Dowlais Iron Company had important iron-mining interests in Spain and this had encouraged many Spanish people to come to Dowlais. A number of them lived in Pen-y-wern, where there were two streets of whitewashed single-storey houses which were very Spanish in appearance. Perhaps surprisingly, relatively few of the Spaniards were fervently Catholic. As a result of all this mixing of incomers – English, Irish, Spanish and others – the language used in everyday parlance was English, and this was particularly true of the younger generation. Many young people regularly attended a Welsh chapel and heard Welsh spoken at home; but insofar as they thought about it at all, they tended to think of Welsh as a language that was used in chapel and its associated activities and that was spoken by their parents and particularly their grandparents. In my own case it was not until I went to college in Aberystwyth in 1937, when I came into contact with a number of Welsh-speaking students from west and north Wales, that I realized that young people of my age could speak Welsh freely with one another as though it was the most natural thing in the world. It shamed me into making serious efforts to improve my own command of the language.

If, then, the language spoken was mainly English, how could it be said that Dowlais was a very Welsh town? Mainly because of the remarkable grip still exerted by Welsh Nonconformity, whose chapels were still very influential. The Independents (*Annibyn-wyr*) were undoubtedly the strongest denomination. They had four handsome and flourishing chapels, each with a membership of about four hundred or upwards. They not only had the most numerous but also the ablest membership, with a higher proportion of managers, teachers and other professional people in their midst. Then came the Baptists (*Bedyddwyr*) with three quite strong churches of about three to four hundred members each; and some way behind lagged the Welsh Methodists (*Methodistiaid Calfin-aidd*) with three rather smaller churches. It was the sort of pattern of denominational allegiance not untypical of industrial south Wales. The scattered English-language Nonconformist chapels were smaller and much less influential. There were also the Anglican churches, one Welsh-language and two English-language, but, though they numbered among their congregations some of the most respectable and well-to-do citizens, they counted for much less in the life of the town. Nonconformist ministers were in those days highly respected and very powerful figures in the community. Some of them, like the famous Peter Price of Bethania, were widely known in Wales. The one I remember best was W. Ceinfryn Thomas, minister of Hebron, Caeharris. He was there for about forty years and was what might be aptly described as the 'squarson' (squire-cum-parson) of the whole village. His formidable personality was such that he could ordinarily quell the sinners with a single glance. But an amusing anecdote used to be told of his coming out of Hebron one weekday evening and looking across at the Red Bull public house, which stood immediately opposite his chapel, with the two institutions as it were glaring across at one another, each trying to stare the other down and muttering under its breath, 'This town ain't big enough for both of us!' Out of the Bull was staggering one of Mr Thomas's less reliable and more bibulous members. The minister glared at him reprovingly and said sternly, 'Drunk again Davy.' To which he received the beatifically disarming reply, 'And me too, Mr Thomas. Lovely isn't it?'

These chapels were not only the focus of religious attendance and worship on Sunday and in the week; they also dominated social and cultural life. During the sombre years of depression, the degree of consolation and comfort they brought to many who were hard-pressed ought not to be overlooked. Every chapel had its own choir and one of the high spots of the year was the denominational *cymanfa ganu*, held at Easter and prepared for carefully for months beforehand. The only chapel big enough to hold the crowds which converged upon it was Bethania, which must have held about a thousand. The *Annibynwyr* held their *cymanfa* on Easter Monday and the *Bedyddwyr* on Easter Tuesday, and anyone who wanted to get in for the evening session which began at six o'clock needed to be there no later than an hour beforehand. The competition between the two denominations was pretty intense and neither willingly yielded the palm to the other. There was always profound interest in the conductors who were invited, and nothing gave the aficionados greater delight than running the rule over the conductors' performance, preferably with a view to establishing how much more expert their own denomination's man had been. These chapel choirs formed a good preliminary training ground for the more select and accomplished choristers who appeared in the celebrated town choirs – male voice, ladies' and chief choral. There had been a succession of notable conductors in the town from the nineteenth century onwards, and the choirs regularly competed at the National Eisteddfod and sometimes won. Uncontrollable excitement prevailed if a choir won in the 'National' and what looked like half the population of the town turned out to welcome home the conquering heroes or heroines.

Many of the chapels conducted their own annual eisteddfod to encourage the local talent. One of the features of these eisteddfodau was the long line of carefully crafted velvet prize bags, devotedly manufactured by the lady members and stretching from one end of the stage to the other. Other chapels might also have their own dramatic company. Gwernllwyn Chapel was particularly strong in this respect and had two very gifted dramatists among its membership – Brinley Jones and the celebrated Leyshon Williams, uncle to Professor Gwyn Alfred Williams, the historian and a future colleague of mine. I played in Leyshon Williams's company for some years and can honestly say that to come under his direction was a liberal education in itself. But every chapel was keen to 'bring on' its promising youngsters, whether as speakers, singers, reciters, or whatever. There must be dozens of people who owe the chapel a profound debt for this kind of early apprenticeship which encouraged their talents.

On the other hand, it would be seriously misleading to give the impression that Nonconformity and the puritanical trends associated with it completely coloured social life. Far from it! Even among many Nonconformists themselves there were strong attractions to more worldly pursuits and forbidden delights. And of course there were a great many others who never came under the sway of Nonconformity at all. Some years ago, a Welsh sociologist, David Jenkins, described two Welsh lifestyles, the first of which he called 'Buchedd A' (Lifestyle A) and the other 'Buchedd B' (Lifestyle B). The former he characterized as conventional respectable Nonconformist existence, with its careful avoidance of the grosser earthly sins. The latter he portrayed as 'living a life in the world', a more carefree existence, with indulgence in drink, gambling and possibly even an adulterous dip on the side. It was a useful distinction, but it overlooked the point that 'Buchedd A' and 'Buchedd B' might coexist in the same family, with father possibly to be typecast as 'Buchedd B' and mother as 'Buchedd A', or again that even 'Buchedd A' people might nevertheless retain some of the traits of 'Buchedd B'. Perhaps this can be illustrated from the experience of the chapel I attended. We always had two tea parties in the year: one was the Sunday school tea party, the grander of the two, which used to go to Barry or Porthcawl, while the other was the Band of Hope tea party. It invariably went to Vaynor on the Thursday of Whit week. Ironically enough, at the Band of Hope tea party the children always had their tea at the Church Tavern, the pub just outside Vaynor Church. And, 'tell it not in Gath, publish it not in the streets of Askelon', some of the older men celebrated in the evening with a drink or two, and not of lemonade, in the Church Tavern. But, then, my Aunt Mary, a rabid teetotaller, saw nothing inconsistent with her temperance principles in brewing homemade wines of stunning alcoholic potency.

Mention of the Church Tavern is a reminder that Dowlais was a town with an extraordinarily large number of public houses. The iron industry had always been a proverbially thirsty one, and the coal industry not markedly less so. Those parched gullets still needed regular laving even in the days of the depression. A good deal of fairly heavy drinking undoubtedly went on, but there was nothing like the unrestrained violence and the yobbish behaviour which tends to accompany indulgence in alcohol nowadays – I do not remember anything to parallel contemporary 'lager louts'. It is difficult to measure these phenomena on the basis of personal experience only and the memory can be fallible, but I have no recollection of violence and thuggery being anything like as acute a problem as it appears to be now.

There were two cinemas in the town which must have transported thousands from their grim existence in the real world to the tinsel and glitter of Hollywood's fantasies. The Victoria

Cinema, always known as 'the Cinema', was a ramshackle old barn of a place, whose seats consisted mainly of uncomfortable long wooden benches. The projector had a nasty trick of breaking down and bursting into flames. At that point, the whole establishment was hastily evacuated. Then, when the fire had been brought under control, the clients were shepherded back in. There was little in the way of crowd control and for every twenty who left about thirty or forty came back in. But that was presumably cheaper and more manageable than refunding admission prices. A discreet silence was always maintained about fire regulations and public safety.

Sports and games of all kinds were played with immense enthusiasm and gusto. Association football rather than rugby was the most popular game. Cricket was widely played in summer, in spite of the difficulty of finding strips of flat ground and spells of fine weather. Tennis, bowls, boxing, swimming, quoits, greyhound racing, pigeon fancying and other sports and pastimes all had their devotees, and were regularly reported in picturesque detail in the *Merthyr Express*. The interest in games and, indeed, many other matters, was intensely localized. The league of local football teams could count on the loyalty of passionate supporters. Some of the matches were keenly contested and none evoked more bitter rivalry than the contests between the local equivalents of Glasgow Rangers and Glasgow Celtic: Dowlais United (known to one and all as the 'Bont') and St Illtyd's (invariably referred to, at least by the irreverent Protestants, as the 'Paddies' or 'Plant Mari').

Interestingly enough, the issue that was bringing the Welsh and Irish closer together was politics, especially the growing popularity of the Labour Party among both groups. Radical political attitudes had been characteristic of the district since the early nineteenth century. Popular stories about such folk heroes as Dic Penderyn, Lewsyn yr Heliwr and Morgan Williams had been handed down since the Merthyr Riots of 1831. One of my most vivid recollections of the General Strike of 1926 is of my grandfather telling me about how governments had always wanted to keep working people in subjection and how the people had struck for liberty, as he put it, nearly a hundred years earlier. Later on, of course, the ever-to-be-remembered Henry Richard had sealed the victory of the Liberal cause, and his kind of politics had ruled the roost more or less unchallenged for many years. But from the early decades of the twentieth century Merthyr became one of the cradles of Labour politics. It had sent to Parliament as one of its representatives no less a luminary than Keir Hardie, that early hero of socialism. The slump of the twenties and thirties, and the acute suffering which accompanied it, added immensely to the appeal of socialism. It was difficult for anyone who had lived in that atmosphere for long not to become intensely left wing in sympathy. The inclinations of most people in that direction were made all the stronger by the rise of the horrifying philosophies of Fascism and Nazism on the Continent. All the same, it was perhaps testimony to the per-sistently strong influence on us of the Liberal tradition that very few were attracted all the way to communism or Marxism. It was democratic socialism that appealed to most people. It was that which seemed to represent the projection on to the national and international stage of that deep inherent sense of brotherhood, shared values and a longing for a fairer and more just order of society that lay at the very heart of our communal life.

II

Early schooldays

A short time back, I had occasion to drive from the junction on the Heads of the Valleys road down into Dowlais along Pant Road. It was dark, and I could not see too clearly, but enough to realize that major changes had taken place since I had last gone down that way. There were many new houses; and some familiar landmarks, like the old Caeracca Bridge, had disappeared. Then to my utter amazement and intense dismay, as I looked in the direction where my old school had been, my unbelieving eyes saw nothing. I realized with an awful shock that all the old school buildings had disappeared and the site had been cleared. I felt bereft! A whole slice of my past existence had been cut away without my even being aware of it. A sharp stab of *hiraeth* went through me. My mind flashed back seventy years and more to the happy early schooldays I had spent there, the teachers who had set me on my way, and the boys and girls who had been my classmates. In one sense, of course, it makes very little difference that the buildings have now gone, because the memories still remain with me, remarkably sharp and vivid after all this time. For seven years, between 1924 and 1931, from the age of four until eleven, next to my home that school had loomed largest in my life.

Looking back now, the first thing that strikes me is what a long way it was for a child, especially in the infants' school, to have to walk from Francis Street in Dowlais, where we lived, to Pant School. It was about a mile each way in the morning, at lunchtime and in the afternoon. Four miles every day was quite a stint, but we never seemed to think much of it when we were children. I suppose we belonged to an age which was accustomed to walking. None of our parents had cars; the nearest thing to private transport in our circle was a costermonger's horse and cart, and he had better things to do with his conveyance than taking us to and from school in it. Public transport of a sort did exist in the shape of buses; but they were very few and far between and not at all convenient, even if we could have afforded the fares.

So we made our way along the main road to the school, unescorted except for some of the older children who obligingly kept an eye on us. Not that there was a great deal of traffic: an occasional van or car, and many more horses and carts. There was also the railway which crossed the road, along which heavy works engines puffed their laborious way, followed by their retinue of coal trucks. The worst hazards – at least as far as I was concerned – were the regular processions of livestock that used to come galloping down the road on their way to the slaughter-house. Their accompanying herdsman always seemed to be an unconscionable distance behind them, and his excitable, barking dogs were more calculated to drive the animals into a frenzy than to their destination. I sometimes felt as though I was facing a Wild West-type stampede of lively bullocks. Many a time I remember pressing myself against the wall so as to squeeze as far as I could out of the path of these fearsome beasts! In retrospect, I suspect that the wretched animals were more scared than I was.

Ordinarily, there were many things along the route to attract the attention of curious youngsters. As we approached the open country between the limits of Dowlais and the beginnings of Pant, we came first to a series of tin sheds, which housed a miscellany of animals and vehicles. Outstanding among them were Tommy Axhorn's splendid team of Belgian bays. These magnificent horses were the pride and joy of Tommy, our local undertaker. He loved exercising, washing, grooming and generally titivating his handsome horses and his funeral conveyances. We used to view these performances with great interest, offering admiring, or sometimes critical, comments for

Tommy's benefit. He was an unusually tolerant man, who would put up with the unsolicited observations of lively kids with infinite good humour. But when the bays, replete with funeral plumes, and the cabs were turned out in all their glory for a funeral, we could only stand in unabashed admiration.

A short way further on, the railway from the works crossed the road to arrive at the public weighing machine. There, I was fascinated by the massive shire horses, with their fine, intelligent heads, powerful hindquarters and shaggy fetlocks. As they drew their heavily laden, old-fashioned carts, I always felt they had a look of infinite patience on their dignified, unmoving faces. Their names always interested me; for the most part, the nomenclature was pretty unimaginative: 'Ben', 'Stout', 'Taff', with an occasional more exotic one like 'Emperor' or 'Champion'. With the closing down of the Dowlais Works in the late 1920s, all this activity came to an end.

The ordinary passenger line continued up towards Pant, parallel with the road. It carried on to Pant Halt and eventually to the intriguingly named Pant Aerial Station. (I never did discover, now I come to think of it, where the 'Aerial' came from.) This was a Great Western line, and just before it arrived at Pant Halt it crossed over the LMS line which made its way on to Abergavenny. The LMS had its own stop at Pantysgallog Halt. Even as a child, it struck me as very odd that a little place like Pant had no fewer than three stations. The LMS line was a source of great delight to us. The train used to emerge from a tunnel just below the school amid a great cloud of steam and it belched its way furiously up the slight gradient, coming to an abrupt halt at Pantysgallog, as though exhausted after its manful efforts. Conversely, it used to leave the Halt in the opposite direction very stealthily and sidle down the gradient towards the tunnel surprisingly quietly, as if it had every intention of taking the tunnel unawares. We used to love standing behind the hedge alongside the line to observe its antics, or, better still, on the bridge over the line to immerse ourselves in the clouds of steam that enveloped us like incense. But Pantysgallog is inseparable, in my mind, from memories of blissful summer picnics in Pont-sarn and Vaynor, one stop down the line.

The other line that went up through Ponsticill towards the Beacons had similar associations, but this time with excursions to such havens of delight as Dol-y-gaer, Torpantau and Tal-y-bont. That Brecon and Merthyr line was the subject of endless scurrilous stories amongst us, on account of the leisurely pace at which the trains proceeded along it. One anecdote told of a guard trying to persuade a man picking blackberries near the line to board the train. 'No thanks,' demurred the reluctant customer, 'I'd like to oblige you, but I'm in a hurry today.' Another reported an exasperated passenger exploding with rage when he got to Merthyr. 'If I'd been travelling a hundred years ago I'd have got here faster.' 'Ah, well,' commented a phlegmatic porter, 'you can't expect any better – it's the same engine.'

Around the school were open fields, with a couple of farms within a stone's throw. They bore their ancient and attractive Welsh names. On the one side was Cwmrhydybedd (The valley of the ford of the grave). It was an appealing, if gloomy, name, and nobody seemed to know whose grave it was. The farmer there was a man called Eddie James, and he delivered our milk every morning. He looked every inch a farmer: about average height but very powerfully built, with a ruddy, weather-beaten face. I made a friend of him for life by persuading him to buy a raffle ticket, on the strength of which he won a fine gold watch. On the other side was a very old farm, which has now disappeared; even in those days there were houses and a railway on three sides. Its name was 'Caerhaca' (The field of the rake), though it was ordinarily spelt 'Caeracca'. The farmer, Siencyn Richards, was quite a character, and his son, Glyn, who was in school with me, was even more of a lad. Pant still preserved a number of the charming old Welsh names which went back to a pre-industrial era. There was Pantysgallog (Hollow of the thistles), yr Hafod (Summer dwelling), Pantcadifor (Hollow of Ifor's seat), Garth (Enclosure), Tai'r Efail (Houses of the smithy) and so on. The local authority had the wit to name some of the streets on their post-1918 housing estates with Welsh names like Rhodfa (Avenue) or Heol y Bryniau (The road to the hills).

The existence of the farms in the immediate vicinity of the school was a reminder to us of the farming life and the agricultural seasons, although we were living in an essentially industrial town. Not that you could entirely escape the industrial influence, even on a farm. Cwmrhydybedd must have leased some of its fields to the Guest, Keen and Nettlefold's Company to enable it to graze its horses. On a post erected near the road stood a menacing notice, which read: 'Guest, Keen and Nettlefold's Ltd. Trespassers will be strictly prosecuted. By order of the Board.' I can still feel that tremor of anxiety going through me as I read those threatening words. They conveyed an image to my childish mind of a group of stern-faced, elderly men, all with dark suits, wing collars and heavy gold watch-chains, sitting round a table. I seemed to see a trembling miscreant brought before them to be threatened with all sorts of dire punishments too awful to contemplate! If that notice was meant to terrify the unwary, it certainly succeeded in my case.

Of my earliest days in school I have only the haziest recollection. I remember my mother telling me much later that I did not want her to come with me to school; I must have thought that would have been unbearably *infra dig*. I wanted to go along with the other children in case I should be regarded as a 'mama's boy'. The risk was all the greater since I was an only child. I suppose there must have been some language difficulties, because, at that stage, I spoke mostly Welsh and my knowledge of English was distinctly sketchy. Hardly any of the rest of my companions spoke any Welsh, so communication may have been something of a problem. But I must have been able to make myself understood and grasp what was being said to me, because I do not remember any difficulties or misunderstandings, except on that memorable occasion when the girl next door, who was some years older than I was and had constituted herself my unofficial guardian, was trying to get me to look at the cows up on the hill and translated 'up on the hill' as 'lan llofft' (upstairs). I confess that I was for a moment pretty puzzled. In the school itself, however, at least three of the teachers would have been able to help me by speaking Welsh. They were all ladies, and all of them were very kind. There were the Miss Morgans – always distinguished as 'Miss Morgan Fat' and 'Miss Morgan Thin'. The former was, indeed, a comfortably upholstered lady, jolly and good-natured. I was a bit of a favourite with her, though I did not altogether care for the way she rather enjoyed hugging me. The other Miss Morgan was much more sparely built and rather austere-looking, though I must say I always found her kind-hearted. As if one pair of teachers with the same name was not enough, the other two on the staff were both called Jones. One was 'Miss Jones the Governess', who was the headmistress, and the other was Miss Winnie Jones, who was an extremely good pianist. They were all very well adapted to infants' school teaching and they created a lovely warm atmosphere in the school.

I cannot truthfully pretend to remember much of what they taught me. I recall, of course, the solemn intoning of the tables – 'twice one is two, twice two are four', and so on. I didn't like 'sums' much and was not very good at them, nor am I still! But I do recall the joy of learning to read and what immense pleasure it gave me to be able to do so. I was an avid reader from an early age. I remember better the wide range of games we used to play in the yard: 'touch', 'fox and hounds', 'hide and seek', 'highbacks' (leapfrog) and many others. What comes back to me more vividly than almost anything else is one of the favourite games we played in the open space that ran around all the school buildings. This we used as a kind of DIY running track. We would divide up into two teams, captained by the two biggest and strongest boys – two heroes called Frank Jennings and Clifford Sims. Frank was my 'captain' and I hero-worshipped him. The teams were roughly equal in attainments, and we would take it in turns, one from each team, to run around the yard in opposite directions, in a sort of glorified relay race. As I was one of the slowest runners, my turn always came near the end. That left me in a fever of anxiety, hoping that some of the stronger runners in my outfit would have built up enough of a lead to ensure that I would not have the humiliation of ending up last. It did not always work.

The great wide world outside did not impinge very much on our innocent pursuits. What Thomas Gray wrote of the pupils of Eton College might equally well have been said of us:

> The little victims play.
> No sense have they of ills to come,
> Nor care beyond today.

But even then, there were some events which created infinite excitement among us. One was Cardiff City's appearance in the Cup Final. I do not believe any of us knew very much about Cardiff City's footballing champions, but we were all passionately partisan in our support of them. The delight we experienced in their victory over Arsenal was quite intoxicating. If, as was widely rumoured, the Welshman who kept goal for Arsenal had deliberately let the ball into his net, then I am afraid our biased opinion was: 'So much the better.' Another sporting contest which aroused great concern was the heavyweight match between Gene Tunney and Jack Dempsey. We knew even less about these two gladiators than about Cardiff, but we were deeply divided this time in our allegiance. Some were dedicated to Dempsey, others to Tunney. I was myself a Dempsey man and was disconsolate when he lost. Another bitter disappointment to me was when the Welshman, Parry Thomas, lost world land-speed record to Malcolm Campbell. I had two toy racing cars: one a model of 'Babs' (Parry Thomas) and the other of 'Bluebird' (Campbell). When I 'raced' them against each other, 'Babs' invariably triumphed.

A very different event that we all knew about and discussed earnestly was the General Strike of 1926. There were all sorts of rumours flying around about soldiers being brought in, what their role and that of the police would be, and what sort of injuries they might inflict. In a working-class area, our sympathies were very much on the side of the strikers. My grandparents (Tadcu and Mamgu) lived round the corner from us and I used to call in there on my way home from school. My grandfather had in his younger days been a collier, but had had to give up work underground because it affected his eyesight so badly. His reaction to the news about the soldiers interested me very much. 'Oh!' he said in deeply resentful tones, 'the government has always been doing that sort of thing.' Then he went on to tell me in graphic terms the story of Dic Penderyn and the Merthyr Riots of 1831, and how soldiers had been sent to Merthyr by the government of the day 'to shoot innocent people', as he put it. It was my first lesson in local social history; not exactly unbiased, perhaps, but it fired my imagination and I never forgot it. At that time I was my grandparents' only grand-child and I was greatly indulged, not to say spoiled, by them. It was my practice to call in on them briefly on my way home from school to see what they were having for dinner (it was years before the term 'lunch' entered my vocabulary). Then I went on home to see what Mother had prepared, and if I did not fancy it as much as what they were having at Mamgu's I would go back to my original port of call and eat with them. My mother was a superb cook but, even so, there were some kinds of meals which appealed to me much less than others.

I adored both my grandparents and I loved spending time with them. My grandfather was a very good singer, and in his boyhood had been bosom friends with the celebrated Dowlais musician, Harry Evans. In later life, Harry was rather cross with Tadcu because he would not take musical training more seriously. But he took it seriously enough to practise regularly at home, and there were few things I liked better than to listen to him rattle off some of his favourite arias. As a result, I acquired a reasonable working knowledge of many of the favourite baritone solos from operas and oratorios – 'Total Eclipse', 'It is Enough', 'Honour and Arms', 'O Ruddier than the Cherry', as well as old Welsh favourites like 'Merch y Cadben' (The Captain's Daughter). But the one I liked best of all was the 'Toreador's Song' from *Carmen* – not only the rousing and dramatic aria itself, but also the narrative of the opera as supplied by my grandfather. He was a highly intelligent man, who made a point of studying the words very carefully and, better still, of acquiring a knowledge of the story and the dramatic situation unfolded in the opera or the oratorio. I think the version he gave me of the amorous Carmen's *affaires* was suitably edited for a youthful listener, but I found the whole story very gripping. Some fifty years later, my wife and I visited Seville. As we stood on the bank of the River Guadalquivir opposite the main entrance to the bullring, I gazed wistfully at the charming little statue of Carmen that stands there. It took me back immediately to those occasions when I listened spellbound to my grandfather, as I was first being introduced to that young *femme fatale*'s tragic career by him all those years before.

Grandfather James Evans.

My grandmother, like my grandfather, had a keen ear for music and a good voice, as indeed did my mother and all her family. It was they who, unbeknown, first planted in me a deep love for music, especially for the human voice, which I have treasured all my life. As I have got older, I have become more and more dependent on the joy and solace that music can bring. I was also fortunate that my grandparents, like my parents, had many books around the house; far more, I think, than were usual in many working-class homes at that time. I was an eager and voracious reader, and they encouraged me to be so. My father, particularly, enjoyed reading and he readily shared his love of it with me, though I have to admit that many of the books in which he delighted – weighty theological tomes – were not altogether to my taste. I much preferred it when he brought novels or travel books home from the library. One of the features of my grandparents' little private 'lending library' was that they had a number of the classical novels of the nineteenth century on their shelves – works by Dickens, Scott, Thackeray, *John Halifax Gentleman*, *The Last Days of Pompeii* and the like. I would not want to suggest that I read these while I was in the infants' school, but I certainly did from about the age of seven or eight onwards.

By that time I had moved up to the 'big school'. How well I remember the staff in the junior school, especially those who taught me, but also many of those who did not. The headmaster then was J. Moseley Jones, a short, sturdily built man, with twinkling eyes, a bald head and a rosy-apple complexion. He was a delightful personality, who retained his youthful sense of mischief until his death at the age of ninety. He retired within two or three years of my coming into the school, and was succeeded by a man of very different type – George Brown, tall, strict, rather austere and forbidding. Most of us found the contrast between him and Mr Jones a bit painful, and we went in great awe of Mr Brown. The first of my class teachers was Richard ('Dick') Humphreys. He was a nice man in many respects, but he had had a very bad time in the First World War and his temper could be a bit fragile. He and I normally got on very well, but one day, he blew his fuse and threw a book at a boy sitting in front of me. Wisely, the intended victim ducked, and the book struck me on the side of the face. I am sure that Dick was more upset by the incident than I was, but my mother was understandably more put out than anyone. She always insisted for years afterwards that, whenever I was tired or unwell, the mark used to show up on my face. I think if she had not reminded me I should probably have forgotten the incident long ago.

Among the other men on the staff, not one of whom actually taught me, were Edward Chapman, Goronwy Griffiths and Goronwy Williams. Griffiths was a lively, athletic figure and a keen tennis player. Williams was a shorter, stouter man, with a most genial smile. I always liked him very much, perhaps because he made a great fuss of me as one of the few who could speak Welsh to him. I was also good at reciting, and he liked getting me to perform for him. I was genuinely sorry to see him leave when he was promoted to a headship in another school.

There were two women who taught me: Miss Lilian Webb in Standard Two and Miss Gwladys Davies in Standards Three,

Four and Five. So much emphasis used to be placed on the 'scholarship' class in those days that it was the practice in Pant to provide greater continuity by having the same teacher to take the class through for two or three years. I could hardly have been more fortunate in my teacher. Miss Davies was in early middle age, with an air of calm, natural authority. There were never any discipline problems, nor any suggestion of the use of the cane. She had an instinctive gift for imparting knowledge in a thorough, but interesting, fashion. While she made sure that we were all thoroughly drilled in 'sums' and 'composition', both of which made up the staple fare of the scholarship examination, she obviously took a much broader and more humane view of what education was supposed to be concerned with. She interested us in all sorts of wider topics and would, for example, encourage us to read Arthur Mee's *Children's Newspaper*. She was also very keen to get us to express ourselves effectively – orally and in writing. I remember, too, how she occasionally took us to the rare Shakespearean productions that came to the Temperance Hall in Merthyr. I owe her an enormous debt, and I held her in the highest esteem and affection. The one thing that surprises me is that, although she spoke Welsh very well herself and regularly attended Gwernllwyn Welsh Independent Chapel, I do not recall her ever teaching us any Welsh. Admittedly, most of the children in the class knew little or no Welsh, and that may have convinced her that there was not much point in trying to teach it. The other consideration may have been that it would not have helped us at all in our preparation for the 'scholarship' examination, and might even have served to distract our attention.

That 'scholarship' loomed large in our lives, of course. But, on looking back now, I am not at all sure that it dominated our existence to the extent that critics of the old system have claimed it did. I still remember very vividly the day of the actual examination. Those of us who wanted to enter the 'Castle' School had to go to Cyfarthfa Castle in Merthyr to sit the examination, and appropriate arrangements were made to transport us there in good time. The grandiose setting of that mock-medieval castle in which the Crawshays had once lorded it was rather off-putting, with its tall, crenellated towers and its high ceilings. To make matters more terrifying, as the first part of the examination was proceeding during the morning, there was a violent thunderstorm, hardly calculated to concentrate the young aspirants' minds on the serious academic business in hand. It certainly was not a very propitious ambience for me, because most of that session was taken up with arithmetic, which was, at best, not my forte.

We lunched in the school canteen, and I found myself sitting next to a senior prefect presiding at the head of the table. He was very amiable and he conversed freely with us in an effort to make us feel at home, I imagine. His name, I discovered, was Vivian Davies, and I think he must have been about eighteen years of age. With his fresh complexion, neatly combed and brilliantined fair hair and dashing plus fours, he seemed to me to be a veritable demigod. I had always been under the impression that only the very smart and well-to-do wore clothes as modish as that! Imagine how much further his stock went up in our estimation when we learned that he played rugby and cricket for the school, represented it at athletics and intended to go on to college. It is odd how much detail one recalls from an encounter that could not have lasted more than about three-quarters of an hour.

Back in, then, to the afternoon session, when my spirits were raised notably by the requirements of the essay and the questions on general knowledge. I thought I might have made some amends for the less-than-brilliant mathematical performance of the morning. I emerged, feeling that, with a bit of luck, I might just scrape in somewhere in the lower half of the list of successful candidates. We now had to find our way home, no transport having been arranged for us. I, with two of my closest friends, Ron Evans and Arthur Kenvin, proceeded to catch a tram running from Cefn to Pontmorlais and there caught another tram up to Dowlais. It took us an age to complete that odyssey, and I began to have some worries about whether it would take as long as that to get home every day in the event of my eventually going to Cyfarthfa School.

In due course, the results of the fateful test were made known. To no one's surprise, my friend Ron Evans topped the list for the whole of the borough. He was an extraordinarily able and versatile boy, who was to go on to pursue a very distinguished academic career. Very much to my own surprise, I found that I had come next on the list. I could only conclude that the essay and the general knowledge questions had compensated for what I knew perfectly well had been a distinctly indifferent showing on the 'sums'. Still, there it was; I was now set for the next stage in my educational pilgrimage. The cloud-capped towers of Cyfarthfa Castle Grammar School beckoned.

III

Life in 'the Castle'

The intense sense of excitement and anticipation that I experienced during those summer months before starting in Cyfarthfa Castle Grammar School – 'the Castle', as we all knew it – in September 1931 is as fresh now as it was then. It was seventy years ago, but I vividly recall how keyed up I was about proceeding to a new school, about which I had heard so much from older friends who were already pupils there. I very much wanted to acquire the regalia that would signal that I, too, was a member of that distinguished academy of learning: the navy-blue cap, with its distinctive yellow stripes and the 'Martyr' Tydfil badge; the blazer with its comparable insignia blazoned on the upper breast-pocket; and the blue and yellow tie. Having had them bought for me, I was just a little apprehensive about how soon it was 'proper' for me to wear them. To sport this finery too soon was to run the risk of being regarded as an intolerable 'show-off'. However, the problem was neatly solved for me because I was going to stay with my grandparents, who now lived in Cardiff, for a week or two. There, in the relative anonymity of a big city, I could appear like Solomon in all my glory. Not that anyone paid the slightest attention to me! Then, there was the school satchel. I had never previously had anything to carry to Pant School except a 'copybook', in which I had done my homework; but now I should have textbooks and a variety of exercise books to transport. It is strange how evocative some smells can be – I can never scent new leather without instantly recalling that school bag and the early days at Cyfarthfa. There was also the little tin case of mathematical instruments and the box of coloured pencils which we had been instructed to obtain. My father, bless him, had been very bright at mathematics at school, and he patiently initiated me into the mysteries of using the compasses, the dividers, the set squares and the like. Kindly and helpful as he was, he did not quite succeed in removing the sense of trepidation I felt about whether or not I should be up to making effective use of these formidable-looking instruments. My misgivings were to prove to be all too well founded.

Going to 'the Castle' was a big step forward for an eleven-year-old. For one thing, it was a long way to walk to school; it must have been three to four miles each way, with no convenient transport other than 'shanks's pony'. Cyfarthfa, on the outskirts of Merthyr, was very awkwardly placed for boys and girls from Dowlais and the upper end of the borough. It was not so bad going to school in the mornings, downhill all the way; but coming back uphill between 4.15 and 5.30 in the afternoon, after a tiring day of lessons, was another story. We did, though, have a lot of fun en route; there was quite a crowd of us going down and coming home together, including a very lively contingent from Pen-y-wern, with whom we used to link up. One of the strange ironies that comes back to me clearly now is that there were a number of boys who had been in Pant School with us who had chosen to go to the other secondary school, the 'County', that is, the Merthyr Intermediate School. We remained on excellent terms with them personally, in spite of the intense rivalry that prevailed between the two schools. The annual rugby matches between the schools were tense encounters, not because there was any violence between the teams or the spectators, but on account of the furious, and totally biased, partisanship on both sides. However, I do remember one very distressing occasion when the two sides played. A member of the 'County' team, a youth called Jimmy Doherty, who was an especially good player and had already been 'capped' for the Welsh Secondary Schools, collapsed and later died. The news cast a desolating sense of sadness over us all, and we slunk away

*G.W. in Cyfarthfa Castle Grammar
School, aged twelve.*

from the ground, glum and dispirited, in almost total and unbelieving silence.

Cyfarthfa Castle, I need hardly mention, is an impressive pile.
It was built on the basis of the vast fortunes made by the
Crawshay family of ironmasters and was intended to emulate
those medieval fortresses built by the landed aristocrats so as to
give the *nouveaux riches* industrialists the style and status they so
ardently coveted. Its huge size, tall towers and massive walls
made it one of the most impressive buildings I had ever seen – it
looked more like a palace than a school to my ingenuous eyes.
The high, large rooms and long, rambling corridors made me feel
thoroughly insignificant, even after I had become more familiar
with them. But the feature which made the most lasting impression on me was the surrounding park. I still count it a piece
of remarkable good fortune that I spent many of my most
impressionable years in such an exquisitely attractive setting. All
the more so, because its barbered lawns and luxuriant flower-
beds were in such stark contrast to the wild, bare, empty hill
and moorland around my home. Both landscapes, startlingly

different from one another as they were, held their deep-seated fascination for me. I am not sure that I realized at the time just how profound a mark they were leaving on me, but the emotion has often been remembered in tranquillity since then. Oddly enough, some years ago, I revisited Cyfarthfa for the first time for many years. We drove out of the park as dusk was falling on a warm, idyllic summer evening. As we went slowly down the slope towards the gate at the Cefn end of the park, the sight of the gentle, grassy incline down in the direction of the lake, absolutely still and flat, brought back a flood of nostalgic memories of the hours that I had spent around there in days gone by. I recalled especially the times when we had been out in the rowing boats on the lake, sitting as still as we could, and watching as the fish swam close, eager to snap up the bits of bread – saved for the purpose from school dinners – that we threw to them. On one all too memorable occasion, I became too eager and fell overboard in my enthusiasm. Dampened in more senses than one, I was dispatched to the caretaker's house and wrapped in a blanket as my clothes dried out.

Behind the castle were the woods, which changed their garb and their colours with the passing seasons; there, when autumn came round, we, like needy peasants, garnered nuts, especially the sweet chestnuts that grew in abundance, to stuff ourselves with. There were small pools, too, that often froze solid in winter and so could safely be slid upon. In another part of the park was a charming old bandstand, where I always longed to hear a brass band playing but never achieved my ambition. Birds nested in profusion in the surrounding bushes; and we searched for their nests, often unintentionally scaring the unfortunate inmates away by our over-solicitous curiosity. Mention of curiosity reminds me of that unforgettable morning when, as we walked along the drive to the castle, looking down over the grassy slope, we saw, to our utter astonishment, two elephants and a giraffe grazing content-edly. We found it difficult to believe our eyes. Only later did we learn that a circus had arrived in town overnight and had temp-orarily taken up residence in the park. These delights of the park were secrets best known to those of us who were 'dinner boys', boys who could not get home and had to stay in school for lunch.

When I first arrived in Cyfarthfa, one of the things that struck me most forcibly was how grown-up the prefects and sixth-formers seemed to be. They appeared to be – indeed were – young men. Of course, they were seventeen or eighteen years of age, but they seemed unbelievably mature to a little boy of eleven. When I saw them turn out at rugby, or cricket, or swimming, their size, strength and physical prowess seemed to be almost more than human. To me, there did not seem to be any appreciable difference between them and some of the younger members of staff. When I first went to assembly in the hall in the morning, I actually thought that two or three of the younger masters, who stood on the outer fringes of the serried ranks of the teaching staff, were senior pupils co-opted to help in keeping order until, a little later, some of those same 'pupils' appeared in the classroom to teach us. The masters were a varied group, from senior figures in their sixties, like the senior master, Sam Adams or Harry Evans ('Sheepy'), down the ranks to the newest recruits, like Havard Walters who is, I am glad to say, still alive and well. They all had their nicknames, some of which showed very little imagination, and others of which left me somewhat baffled by their relevance to the individual concerned. Adams, or 'Sammy', was a short man but a figure of great natural dignity who could command order in the mornings by a single clap of the hands and a quelling glance over the bridge of his Roman nose. His favourite phrase was 'there will be a weeping and a wailing and a gnashing of teeth', a threat more honoured in the utterance than the fulfilment thereof.

There were, I remember, three Davieses among the masters, which could at times cause a measure of confusion. There was the headmaster, D. J. Davies, known to us all as 'the Boss', E. L. Davies ('Dai Bump') and J. E. Davies ('Johnny Stinks'), who lived on a farm and used to appear on wet mornings, of which there were many, resplendent in shiny brown leather farmer's leggings. Early on in my career I was sent to the staffroom with a message for 'Dai Bump'. I had enough sense to know that I should ask for Mr Davies, but when I had knocked the door and was asked, 'Which Mr Davies do you want?', I was stumped. I thought that if we called him 'Dai Bump' his Christian name must be 'David' and, politely, as I supposed, I asked for 'Mr David Davies'. Luckily for me, it was one of the younger and more good-humoured members of the staff who had asked me the question, and he rather charmingly corrected me, saying, 'I think it must be Mr *E. L.* Davies you want'. To my shame, E. L. Davies's mother and sister were members of the same chapel which my parents attended, so in all conscience I ought to have known what his initials were. E. L. Davies was in many respects an idiosyncratic character and was famous, among other things, for being the owner of a motor car – a very rare possession in those days. It rejoiced in being a 'Bean' by make and, not surprisingly, was known to us disrespectful boys as the 'Has Been'.

We were now being brought into contact with not only a much larger and more diverse range of teachers but also with a wider spectrum of subjects. I liked most of the new subjects we now encountered, though I still found some difficulty with mathematical topics. What I did note, however, was that it was not so much subjects that appealed to me as the individuals who taught them. I still recall that there were one or two masters with whom I was never at cross-purposes myself, but who nevertheless used to make me feel extremely nervous. One of them had an unpredictable temper and, when roused, would go white with anger and tremble with rage. It did not happen very often, but I was always scared that one day I would do something that might upset him and he would vent his wrath on me. I know that I did not do very well in the subject he taught, largely because of the uncertainty that he roused in me. I was not all that good at art, either, but I always enjoyed the art lessons with Charlie Holder who, in addition to being our art master, was also curator of the Cyfarthfa Museum and frequently took us into the museum for our art lessons. Because these lessons were so much more relaxed and informal, I think we always rather revelled in being let loose in the museum.

At the end of the second year we had to make a choice of subjects, which virtually entailed choosing between arts and science for the rest of one's school career. In spite of what I said earlier about not being very good at mathematical studies, I had taken well to physics and chemistry and would have liked to pursue them further. But in order to do so I should have been obliged to give up arts subjects, which I liked even better, so I opted for arts. In the sixth form I remember feeling distinctly peeved that I could not study more science. What accounted for this hankering after science was that we, as arts students, were very sensibly required to pursue for two hours a week what was called 'general science'. Oddly enough, it was J. E. Davies who was deputed to guide our uncertain footsteps. In the first two years at school he had taught us physics and, it must be said, not very well. But when it came to general science in the sixth form, he seemed to be an entirely different person. He was not only genuinely interested in the subject but he succeeded in infusing the same interest into us. We talked about Rutherford and the splitting of the atom and its possible implications, about the Curies and the discovery of radium and X-rays, and, most fascinating for me, about Darwin and evolution. It left me, thereafter, with a lively, if undisciplined, interest in science and scientific discovery, which still persists.

However, for good or ill, I had opted for arts subjects, at which I seemed to perform pretty well. I appeared to be good at essay-writing and, rather against my will, was encouraged (I will not say dragooned) into entering essay competitions. I had not much fancied the idea of entering the competitions, but a number of prizes came my way. I must confess to feeling rather chuffed when, having won the *Western Mail*'s St David's Day essay competition, I found myself being photographed, by that newspaper's photographer, receiving the prize from the headmaster in morning assembly. Talking of competitions and performances, I was also considered to be a competent reciter and actor in those days. The school used to have an eisteddfod every St David's Day and also had a lively and active branch of Urdd Gobaith Cymru (Welsh League of Youth). Havard Walters, who taught Welsh, was extremely enthusiastic about the Urdd and, because he was young and good-humoured, we responded readily to this. He was keen that we should avail ourselves of the opportunity of going to the eisteddfodau and the summer camps organized by the Urdd. A memorable occasion was the eisteddfod held at

Colwyn Bay, which we attended as a group shepherded by Mr Walters. We left Merthyr in the small hours and arrived at Colwyn Bay about breakfast time. We were all starving by that time and were taken off to the first available café. About twenty of us, I suppose, were sitting around the table and a gargantuan enamel teapot was dumped in front of Mr Walters. He picked it up, his arms trembling under the sheer strain, and aimed in the direction of the nearest teacup. So heavy was the pot, and so full, that a stream of tea poured out in a long, graceful arc and landed in one of the cups furthest away from him. So the process continued, the most distant cups being filled first, in descending order until he could manage the nearest ones. The Urdd camps, too, were very popular. We had gone to the one at Llangrannog, and one of our number who enjoyed a whiff on the sly had gone into an empty hut for a quick drag. A suspicious *swyddog* (officer) came nosing around the hut. The errant one promptly ducked down under the bed out of sight; but when the *swyddog* threw open the door and called out, 'Pwy sy mewn 'ma?' (Who's in here?), the sinner was unthinking enough to reply, 'Neb' (No one)!

I probably enjoyed my two years in the sixth form best of all. Not that I found it at all easy to choose which subjects to study. The die was already cast in favour of its being an arts course. The difficulty was in deciding which of the arts subjects I should choose. The result of the Senior Certificate level examinations gave me some useful guidance. I had done pretty well in all the subjects I had sat, but had scored the highest marks in English, history, Welsh and geography, so it seemed that I ought to think seriously about 'perming' three out of these four. The most difficult choice lay between Welsh and geography, because in practice it was impossible to study both simultaneously. I liked geography very much and had found the master who taught it particularly stimulating. At this stage in my life, however, I was seriously considering entering the Christian ministry, and I thought that perhaps Welsh would be a more appropriate subject for me. In the end, I settled for English, Welsh and history.

One of the appealing things about the sixth form was that you had reduced your range of subjects to three, which you liked and at which you were reasonably good. Another advantage was that the classes were quite small, and were more like tutorial or discussion groups than the large classes of thirty to thirty-five to which one had been accustomed. Another attractive feature was that you were now allowed a number of 'free periods' in the course of the week which could be used for private reading. It was at this time that I came to realize what a relatively good library the school had, and to make effective use of it. That, in turn, stimulated me to make much more intensive use of the municipal libraries in Merthyr and in Dowlais. It was about the same time that Penguin books began to appear on the market, and I recall with enormous pleasure the thrill of being able to acquire great works like Élie Halévy's *History of England* for sixpence a volume. I became, and have remained, a confirmed Penguin buyer, though they come at rather more than sixpence a time these days. I should not want to try to give the impression that we were always model students, at all times making the best possible academic use of our free periods. We were often given to discussing and arguing fiercely about politics, religion or social problems, as well as many less weighty issues. This, after all, was the mid-1930s, the years when unemployment, depression, Abyssinia, Spain, Manchuria and demonic individuals like Hitler and Mussolini loomed large in all our imaginations. Nor were all our conversations confined to the bounds of the school; we often took the opportunity on warm spring and summer afternoons to continue them – and our lazing – out in the park.

It was the headmaster who taught us European history in the sixth form. If the truth be told, he was not an especially good teacher, but he had a tremendous delight in the subject, which he successfully conveyed to us. Theoretically, we were studying the period from 1763 to 1914, but 'the Boss' had such an absorption, almost amounting to an obsession, in the French Revolution and Napoleon, that we never got much further than 1815. Even so, it was he who introduced me to great historians like H. A. L. Fisher and Albert Mathiez, and also opened my eyes to what superb literary writers like Thomas Carlyle and Charles Dickens had to contribute to our understanding of history. He was also very good at encouraging us to go to the Merthyr Settlement to listen to talks by eminent figures like R. H. S. Crossman, who came there. I owe the headmaster a great debt in that respect as, indeed, I do to Gwilym Williams, who taught us British history. He was always known to the boys as 'Nero', though I have never known quite why, because a less dictatorial or imperialistic type it would be difficult to imagine. Sam Adams was responsible for English. Though he was a rather dry, serious man, without much obvious sense of humour, he was an excellent teacher of the old school. It was he who initiated us into the world of literary criticism, and for the first time in my life I really began to grasp what the poet's art was all about. It was he, too, who opened up to me what a towering genius Shakespeare was and something of the nature of the perennial human problems which he had so searchingly unveiled. I hardly needed any encouragement from Sammy to plunge into the works of the great literary critics he brought to our notice. What I derived enormous stimulation from was the contribution being made to our discussion by a tiny, élite group of third-year sixth-formers, who were back in school preparing to sit for university scholarships.

One of the privileges of being in the sixth form was that you were allowed to venture upstairs to the sacred precincts of the girls' school to study certain subjects. Welsh was one of these. The boys' school on the ground floor and the girls' school on the floor above were kept apart and never the twain were allowed to meet, except for some interchanges of subject at sixth-form level. I mentioned earlier how evocative some smells can be, and the smell of beeswax polish immediately brings back that pungent scent that greeted you as you opened the door that led up to the girls' school. The floors there were highly polished, and the girls were obliged to wear gym shoes and strictly forbidden to wear outdoor shoes while in school. The Welsh mistress, Miss Hettie Morris, was in sharp contrast to the Welsh master I had hitherto known. Whereas he was young, humorous and unusually affable, she was middle-aged, stern and severe. But she was a remarkably thorough and effective teacher, who gave her pupils a penetrating appreciation of the merits of modern and ancient Welsh literature, even if she was a bit too serious-minded for our admittedly frivolous temperaments. I do remember her melting on at least one noteworthy occasion. It was the last lesson in the afternoon, and although it had turned 4.15, when we were supposed to be released, and I could hear the rest of the boys' school making their way home, Miss Morris was insistent on completing the discussion of the subject on which she was engaged: the literary merits of the greatest Welsh hymn-writers. Perhaps because she could see that my gaze and my attention were wandering, she asked me if had a favourite hymn. I replied, in what I have since realized was a world-weary tone, 'Yes I have, Miss Morris. It's

> Mae 'nghyfeillion adre'n myned
> O fy mlaen o un i un.
>
> [My friends are homeward bound;
> going before me, one by one.]

I am surprised I took the risk of giving such a flippant reply; but, in fairness to Miss Morris, she saw the funny side of it and burst into laughter.

Another extraordinary episode which befell us as a Welsh class occurred one day when we were late arriving for a lesson. There were only three of us in the group, and one of us was inclined to be something of a harum-scarum. He was late on this occasion – as indeed he very frequently was – and we were waiting for him to join us before going into the classroom. As he dashed helter-skelter around the corner, Miss A. C. Davenport, the headmistress of the girls' school, was arriving on the scene. I should explain that Miss Davenport was a tall, handsome lady, with an impeccable carriage, beautiful white hair and piercing blue eyes. She was a stickler for dignity and discipline, and was determined that those boys who were allowed to encroach upon her hallowed domain should behave with due decorum – and perhaps a bit more. On this ill-fated occasion, however, neither she nor our colleague could see each other as they approached the corner of destiny. Crash! The latecomer went full tilt into her and both ended up on the floor, sitting on their posteriors and gazing helplessly at one another. I doubt whether Miss Davenport had ever before suffered such *lèse-majesté*; but she was too taken aback to say anything. We hastily stepped forward to help her to her feet, apologizing profusely for the mishap. I think she just could not recover her poise sufficiently to do more than say, in breathless tones, 'See that never happens again.' As if we would!

I left Cyfarthfa a year sooner than I had expected to do. After two years in the sixth form I sat the Higher Certificate examination when I was aged seventeen years and one month. I had always cherished the hope that I might be able to go on to university, all being well, but I had always known that I should have to win a scholarship to be sure of doing so. I had seen many bright boys having to leave school after passing Senior Certificate because their parents were not able to face the costs of maintaining them in higher education. I had imagined that I stood a reasonable chance of passing the Higher Certificate first time, but that if I wanted to win a scholarship I should have to go back to school to improve on my record. So I had made no enquiries about going to university that year. The results of the examination, when they were announced, surpassed my wildest expectations, however. I had been awarded a distinction in history and in Welsh, and a near-distinction in English. Shortly afterwards, I was also told that I had been awarded a state studentship, a Merthyr Borough studentship and the Sir Owen Edwards Scholarship. I was walking around in a mixture of ecstasy and bewilderment, but I still thought I should stick to my original intention of returning to school for another year. I thought then – for that matter I think now – that I really was too young to go to university and was not sufficiently prepared, intellectually or emotionally, for the transition.

I had not, however, counted on the attitude of 'the Boss'. When I went to see him, he was naturally very pleased and warmly congratulated me on doing so well. Then he said, 'Now I think you must change course for the future. I want you to go to the London School of Economics like Aubrey Jones did.' (Aubrey Jones was an outstandingly gifted pupil, who later became an MP and a member of the government as minister of supply.) 'When you come back to school, I want you to drop English and Welsh, and take economics and German instead.' I was quite flabbergasted by this suggestion; I had never studied economics or German, and I did not think I wanted to either, particularly as I should have had to pursue them very largely on my own. I had no idea at that stage whether or not I should be any good at them. I demurred and said that I had hoped to come back to school and extend my reading; that I did not think I was ready to go to university. I do not think that 'the Boss' had expected me to go counter to his wishes, and I had obviously flicked him on an exposed nerve. From then on, the interview deteriorated in tone, and it ended up with him saying, a bit brusquely, 'I don't want you coming back and repeating the subjects you've already done; you'll be far too likely simply to waste your time.' I felt disappointed and a bit aggrieved and said, somewhat sulkily, that I thought I had rather go to university and undertake something I wanted to study than come back to school to do something I had no interest in. I think we might both have exercised rather more patience and restraint.

Anyway, the upshot was that I took myself to the University College of Wales, Aberystwyth. I have more than once asked myself whether or not that was the right thing to have done. Certainly, I was very happy in Aberystwyth, and it worked out very well in the end. In any event, it is impossible to tell what would have happened if I had taken the other path at that cross-roads. Life is not an experiment you can rerun in different circumstances. Dwelling on the might-have-beens serves no useful purpose; I shall never know how things would have turned out. I should just be grateful that my life proved to be as happy and fulfilling as it did.

IV

'The College by the Sea', 1937–1942

The Aberystwyth to which I went in 1937 looked in many respects much the same as it does today. Then, as now, the town was a quintessentially Victorian creation. The long sweeps of the promenade, from the harbour to Constitution Hill, gave expression to the nineteenth- and early twentieth-century zest for fresh sea air – not excluding the dubious aroma of decaying seaweed, which the local people always insisted on designating the 'whiff of ozone'. That promenade was graced with the remains of a medieval castle, a striking war memorial to the dead of 1914–18, the University College and the Theological College next door, the inevitable pier, and a succession of large hotels and boarding houses, all looking expectantly out to sea. Just inland stood the commercial heart of the town, with banks and shops exuding an air of solid prosperity. Along the main thoroughfares had been erected those enormous chapels and churches dedicated to the worship of God (though thoughts in the direction of Mammon never strayed far from the businesslike Cardiganshire minds) and the many temples put up for the devotees of Bacchus, together with the numerous cafés for those of more abstemious disposition.

There have, it is true, been a few notable changes. The harbour has been transformed by the current mania for marinas; thousands of students have long since migrated from 'the College by the Sea' to 'the College on the Hill'; some of the big hotels have been transmogrified into offices; many of the chapels look a bit woebegone and one of the largest has been pulled down; most of the boarding houses no longer admit visitors or students; and contemporary traffic threatens to create arterial sclerosis by its density. Yet Aberystwyth retains much of its relaxed Victorian charm. It is still a rare delight to meander gently along its promenade, especially perhaps in the evening, 'kicking the bar' at its north end, as was our nightly ritual when we were students. The two phenomena I can never dissociate from the 'prom' are its serenely spectacular 'Turner' sunsets over Cardigan Bay and the unbridled fury with which the west winds could blow onshore. I still remember vividly that fearsome winter storm of early 1938, with its mountainous waves and raging blasts, which battered down half the pier and engulfed a large part of the promenade. Nor, conversely, shall I ever forget the peaceful, green surrounding Ceredigion countryside with its unpretentious villages and its entrancing coastline, especially up towards Clarach, Wallog and Borth.

Travel to and from Aberystwyth in pre-war days was also a relaxed and leisurely affair. Cars, of course, were a rare luxury unknown to most students, who had no option but to depend on public transport to get to their destination. Travelling there by train was, by any standards, frustratingly time-consuming and inconvenient. Going from Dowlais incurred at least two changes of train and a tedious journey. It included the proverbially snail-paced peregrination from Carmarthen to Aberystwyth, with its twenty-seven potential stops (some of them 'by request only') over a distance of forty-five miles. A few of these rejoiced in romantic names like Conwil Elvet, Derry Ormond and Caradoc Falls. Arriving at the last-named, one sarcastic fellow traveller commented drily, 'If Caradoc falls here, I wonder if he'll think it worth his while ever getting up again?' It was he who also told me the harrowing traveller's tale of the passenger going in the opposite direction to Carmarthen who, as he alighted there, emitted a great heartfelt sigh of relief and said, 'Well, that's the worst part of the journey over!' When asked whither he was bound, he replied, 'Shanghai.'

It was quicker and cheaper to opt for the bus. At Neath there were always enough Aber-bound students to make it worthwhile for the Western Welsh Company to put on a special bus or buses to transport us. With a busful of students on board there was, as might have been imagined, a good deal of banter and leg-pulling. One unfortunate inspector was always detailed to ensure the 'safe carriage' of the unruly human cargo. The character who comes back to mind was a somewhat officious individual known as Inspector Harris. The poor fellow was utterly devoid of any sense of humour and, worse still, filled with an awareness of the importance of his own responsibility. He was, inevitably, subjected to a choice variety of pranks, suggestions and comments; they served only to make him more pompous and frequently led to threats that the bus would be stopped forthwith. Exasperated almost beyond endurance, he was greeted on one occasion by a voice addressing him in mock-pious clerical tones, 'Brother, have you tried prayer?' It was anything but prayer that he was provoked into trying!

The bus ordinarily made good progress and arrived in Aberystwyth after a journey of some three to four hours. It would have got there sooner but for the statutory 'comfort stop' of half an hour or so in Lampeter. On one memorable occasion I took the opportunity to avail myself of what looked like a partially constructed public convenience. The door shut behind me with an ominous slam and when I tried to get out I found there was no handle on the inside. All that could be seen was a small, circular, glazed porthole. I managed to attract my friend Clem's attention and succeeded in getting him to understand that I was locked in. He went off, presumably to get the key, but it seemed an age before he returned. It was just as well I had not heard the ensuing conversation. The locals told him that the building was part of a new gaol that was being put up and that the custodian of the key was away for a week. Luckily, some frantic toing and froing and hectic enquiries managed to produce a spare key in the police station. I was spared hours of potential self-incarceration.

Unlike many university students at that time, who travelled in daily to their university, those at Aberystwyth were nearly all residential. All the men students lived in 'digs', except for the handful able to live at home. Many of the matrons of the town made an all-year-round living by housing students in the winter months and visitors in the summer. Aber landladies were a formidable breed, accustomed to the ways of students; they were usually good-hearted, but not personages to be trifled with. When I got to Aber I arranged to share digs with another young man from Dowlais, Clem Lewis, with whom I had been close friends at school. He was a year or two older than I was but he was, like me, a 'fresher' in his first year. We were to share rooms for the next three years, and it would have been difficult to find a better 'co-digger' with whom to live. We neither of us knew at first where our digs – Fairlea, Loveden Road – were situated. All we knew was that the house was described as being 'two minutes walk from the prom', so I unhelpfully suggested that perhaps we ought to make for the prom and then walk for two minutes. However, having been directed there by more experienced students, we found Fairlea to be a comfortable house at the eastern end of the town, very close to the Town Hall. The arrangements for us were the same as for most of the men students. We paid ten shillings each a week for our rooms – a sitting room and a bedroom – which we shared. The landlady bought much of our food, for which we paid her, of course, and she also did the cooking. One of the calumnies about Aberystwyth tradesmen that regularly went the rounds was that there were four tariffs for the commodities in their shops: the most expensive for summer visitors, the next for students, a lower one for townspeople and the cheapest of all for townspeople of the same denomination as the shopkeeper.

The women students lived in two hostels on the seafront. The larger of the two, Alexandra Hall ('Alex'), was a great barracks of a building at the extreme north end of the prom, while Carpenter Hall ('Carp') was a much more modest structure about halfway along. The arrangements for men and women to meet still preserved – in theory anyway – a strong Edwardian flavour, and were staid, old-fashioned and strictly regulated. If a girl wanted to go out in the evening she had to sign the late-leave book by midday or would not be allowed out. A man who had arranged to meet a girl had to present himself at the hall and give his own name and the name of the lady he wanted to see. He would be shown into a room to wait while the maid took the message to the young lady and returned with the reply. Any girl student who went out in the evening had to be back by 10 p.m., but was given an extra half-hour on Saturdays. I only once penetrated beyond the waiting room in Alex – when I was in my final year. As president of the Students' Union I was formally invited to lunch there. I thought it was one of the most ghastly meals which it had ever been my misfortune to consume, though Fay, who was later to become my wife, assured me that it was measurably less bad than usual. The warden of the hall, Mrs Guthkelch ('Mrs G.'), was a lady of, to put it mildly, somewhat awe-inspiring visage and disposition. Being absorbed in psychology, she put us through our paces in a series of questionnaires. One of the first questions she asked me was the quite extraordinary query, 'Which would you prefer to have, Mr Williams, a yacht or a baby?' Flabbergasted though I was, I managed to dream up what, even today, I think was a pretty snappy reply: 'As I'm in no imminent danger of acquiring the one or the other, I pass on that one.'

For four out of the five years I spent in Aberystwyth, I lived in Fairlea. Our landlord and landlady there were Tom and Rachel Jenkins, a good-natured and easy-going couple, who looked after their 'boys', as they described us, very well. They were old hands at taking in lodgers, and for years had housed the former college librarian, Richard Ellis. He was an old bachelor and a scholar of some distinction, who had worked for years on the papers of the illustrious Welsh polymath, Edward Lhuyd. Ellis died suddenly, and his friend, the celebrated poet, T. Gwynn Jones, had looked in vain for his writings. Then, one evening in conversation, Tom Jenkins unwittingly let the cat out of the bag as to what had befallen them. 'Oh,' he said, 'when we were clearing up, we found piles and piles of his papers locked away in an old cupboard. I used them to light the fires for months afterwards.'

Rachel, a jolly and well-upholstered lady, some years younger than her husband, hailed from the Rhondda. She was very well meaning but was not much of a cook. One lunchtime, she came to break the news to us that Nipper, their little Sealyham dog, had stolen the chops she had cooked for our lunch and eaten them. The disaster had reduced her to floods of tears. 'There, there', said Clem in soothing tones, 'don't worry, Mrs Jenkins, we'll help you to bury Nipper.'

Her husband, Tom, was the descendant of an old Aberystwyth family, who had lived in the town for three or four generations. He was a tailor by trade and a very good one at that. Though he was about sixty years of age, he had sat cross-legged at his work for so long that he was never happy sitting in a chair but always preferred to squat on his haunches. He was an inveterate smoker of Woodbines – no other cigarette held any appeal for him – and he used to smoke them down to just about the last shred with the aid of a pin, so that his fingertips were almost black with tobacco stains. He had a greater unconscious genius for malapropisms than anyone else I have ever known. Commenting on Richard Ellis, he remarked, 'He was a very nice man, but a bit *concentric* in his habits.' He used to urge us to get on with our *squatting* (swotting) and to *consecrate* (concentrate) for our exams. He referred to the pope, who had just died, as 'lying in state in the *Vacuum*' (Vatican), and was deeply concerned about the *Maggot* Line (Maginot Line), then much in the news, and whether it would be proof against the attacks of the *calvary* (cavalry) with their *banjoliers* (bandoliers). He recounted with enthusiasm units of the fleet *manurin'* (manoeuvring) in the bay, and the convenience of having a telephone *kissock* within yards of the house. One of his most favoured terms was 'pseudo-', which always tripped off his tongue as *persuado-*. Our fellow students found it hard to credit Tom's faculty for mangling the English language until they heard it for themselves.

Much to my dismay, the Jenkinses gave up taking students in my last year, so I had to move to live with two other young men from Welshpool, Ian Puleston Jones (always known as Dan, with whom I had earlier lived in Fairlea) and Rex Lewis, two of the most delightful men I have ever encountered anywhere. We lived in Portland Street in a house belonging to an immensely likeable, middle-aged spinster, Miss Turvey, and her elderly father. Though Turvey *père* was very ancient and feeble, he used to like to go to a neighbouring hostelry called James's Vaults; it was dark, gloomy and thoroughly uninviting. The only comparable bars I have seen were those in the far south-west of Ireland. He was so tottery that when he ventured to James's Vaults, we would have to go and half-carry him home at 10 p.m. One of the things that gave us most pleasure at Miss Turvey's was her ancient wind-up gramophone and her collection of records, notably selections from Gilbert and Sullivan. We played them just about threadbare.

In the late 1930s 'the College by the Sea' numbered no more than about seven to eight hundred students, roughly one-tenth of those who are at Aberystwyth today. Most of them were housed in departments concentrated in the Old College in King Street. There were others in scattered outposts – music and international affairs next door in King Street; geography, educa- tion and modern languages on the front; agricultural depart- ments and zoology were in Alexandra Road opposite the station; further out again was chemistry on the Buarth, and the dairy in Llanbadarn Road. But most people thought of the Old College as the heart and soul of Aber. Built originally as an enormous rambling hotel on the sea front, the college had a charm all of its own. Its central hall, the quad, stretched up to the roof and was ringed by stone balconies. At mid-morning students indulged in the endearing habit of perambulating slowly around in pairs and conversing on an unimaginable range of topics, or else other groups gazed down on them – sometimes idly, sometimes curiously – from the balconies high above. On one of the long sides of the quad were two radiator grills, from one of which the president of SRC or his deputy made the announcements for the day. It is my impression that almost as many marriages were made in that quad as in heaven!

Aberystwyth prided itself on being the University College of Wales and the oldest of the colleges of the University of Wales. To a greater extent than any of the other colleges, it drew its students from all parts of Wales. Nevertheless, there was a well- defined recruitment from the Welsh-speaking western areas of Wales and there was among the students a very large proportion of Welsh-speakers. For the first time in my life I found myself in the midst of many young people of my own age who spoke Welsh to one another in their daily converse as an entirely natural means of communication. I was deeply impressed and made really serious efforts to improve and practise my spoken Welsh. I met with some success, but even to this day I am sure that I do not speak the language as easily and idiomatically as those who spoke it as youngsters, particularly at play and in school with their contemporaries. At the same time I have good reason to be grateful to the college for reawakening my pride in my native language and for implanting in me the desire to speak it as fluently as I could.

I encountered many of these Welsh-speakers in Bethel, the chapel I attended in Aberystwyth. It was in those days very usual for students to attend the chapels in the town. Bethel had two flourishing Sunday school classes – one for men students and the other for women. The former was conducted by Dr T. J. Jenkin, one of the high priests of the Welsh Plant Breeding Station, and the latter by Professor David Evans, professor of German at the college. T. J. Jenkin was a superb Sunday school teacher, a scientist of unimpeachable integrity, religious, moral and intellectual, and an exceptionally wise and broad-minded man. I learnt as much from that class as I did from any of my college lectures.

Nearly all the students at Aberystwyth and, indeed, in the Welsh colleges generally, were the products of the Welsh grammar schools. Many of them were sprung, as I was myself, from working-class families – more, I am sure, than was usually the case in contemporary English universities. I noticed the difference very markedly in 1940, when students from the University College of London were evacuated to Aberystwyth. Most of these were quite obviously of middle-class parentage and more comfortably off than the Aberystwyth students. They were not necessarily any the worse for that, though the differences between the two student bodies were unmistakable.

My earlier misgivings about my own relative immaturity and unpreparedness for university life were soon confirmed. Many of the senior students appeared to me to be vastly more sophisticated and much wiser in the ways of the world than I was then. In my first week this was sharply brought home to me. I had been invited to take part in the freshers' debate in the

Debates Union, the leading college society. In a confused mood of excitement and trepidation, I agreed to do so. One of the speakers on the opposing side was Emyr Humphreys, then a fresher and later to become a celebrated novelist. I still recall his sensitive, intelligent face and his remarkable command of language, wit and argument. Though he was only a year or two older than I, he made me aware of what a raw and callow schoolboy I still was. However, as he, too, was studying history, we became close friends and have remained so ever since. This has not prevented me from being convinced that he has a deeper understanding of life and human beings than I could ever hope to possess.

Emyr was not the only man of literary ability to leave his mark on me. Another member of the college in my first year was the poet, Alun Lewis. At about the age of twenty-three and in his last year, he was already becoming widely known as a poet of distinction. I have never forgotten the first time I saw him without knowing who he was. Even then, with his pale face, black hair and his sad dark eyes, he looked haunted and stricken. I got to know him because he occasionally came to meetings of the History Society. The gap between us in terms of experience and maturity was painfully wide, but he was remarkably kind and patient, however disappointing conversation between us must have been for him. But if ever a man looked doomed to meet a tragic outcome it was he; and I do not think I say that simply in the light of hindsight. Another senior student fated to come to a desperately unhappy end was a man with Dowlais connections – Frank R. Lewis. An exceptionally gifted historian and writer, he took me 'under his wing' and helped me a great deal in the early stages. But in the long run he turned out to be wretchedly miserable and unstable, and ended his days in and out of mental hospitals. Then there was another gifted poet, T. Henry Jones. Though younger than I, Harri looked older. He, too, had that dark, brooding Celtic introversion that was perhaps inevitable in a man of his poetic endowment. He was later to emigrate to Australia where he came to a sad and untimely end.

Aberystwyth had, if anything, an even greater reputation as the centre of literary activity in Welsh than in English. Its newly

Committee of the Celtic Society, Aberystwyth, 1941. Front row: Mary Jones, G.W., J. R. Jones (staff president), Emrys Jones, Auriol Griffiths.

retired professor of Welsh, T. Gwynn Jones, was one of the greatest Welsh poets of the modern era. His younger colleague, T. H. Parry-Williams, was as celebrated a prose-writer as he was a poet. Another member of the department, D. J. 'Gwenallt' Jones, was also emerging as a major figure among the ranks of Welsh writers. Not surprisingly, they attracted many students who themselves aspired to become littérateurs. Leading figures among them were Gwyndaf, already a bardic winner at the National Eisteddfod, David Marks, Dyfnallt Morgan – a Penydarren boy and himself to be a National winner in due course – Eluned Ellis Williams and a number of others. These would-be writers, in Welsh and English, were regular contributors to the college magazine, a bilingual publication of more than average merit, which appeared regularly once a term.

The sporting activities of the college, it need hardly be added, were no less lively than its social life. All the major sports were well patronized: rugby, soccer, cricket, hockey, tennis, athletics and the like. One of the less usual sports, but much enjoyed, was rowing. The rowing club had at its disposal some four-oared boats, which were wheeled round on handcarts from a building near the lifeboat station in Queen's Road. They were taken round to the lifeboat slip on the prom to be launched into the uncertainties of the Cardigan Bay waves. I got hauled in to act as cox for one of the hopeful crews. Among my fellow argonauts, and an exact contemporary of mine as a student, was C. W. L. (Bill) Bevan, later principal of the University College at Cardiff. Bill was more brainy and muscular than average, exceptionally versatile at all sorts of activities, intellectual and athletic. I lost touch with him for many years after the war when he was in Nigeria, but was happy to renew our friendship when he returned to Cardiff in the 1960s.

The highlight of the college year, in cultural no less than sporting terms, was the Inter-college Week, held about the middle of February each year. All four colleges of the university were allowed four days free of lectures and classes to participate in intercollegiate matches and the intercollegiate eisteddfod. It was a week when jollification was possibly even more in evidence than competition. Aber always rather fancied its chances in the eisteddfod. With a strong music department and a whole crop of budding poets and writers, we confidently reckoned to come out on top – though we did not always do so!

One of Aber's privileges most highly esteemed by students was its offer of a limited number of scholarships every summer vacation to enable undergraduates to travel in Europe. To qualify, a student had to have completed at least two years in the college and to have done well academically. In the fateful summer of 1939, the last in which such scholarships were to be offered as it turned out, financed by one of these grants, I set off for France with two companions: John Ll. Edwards, later professor of law at Toronto University, and Evan D. Evans, subsequently principal lecturer in history at Cardiff College of Education. Continental travel was a much less usual activity in those days, and this was the first time that any of us had been to Europe, so it was an unforgettable occasion for us. To make our money last, we hitch-hiked and lived sparsely in youth hostels, thus managing to stay in France for about a month or five weeks.

One thing that became increasingly obvious was that, with detachments of young conscripts around and all kinds of other military preparations in evidence, the French people seemed to have little doubt that we were on the eve of war.

I should not want to give the impression that it was all fun and games and that we did very little academic work. Quite the contrary; most of us were only too aware of the sacrifices that had to be made by our parents to give us the opportunity of being amongst that favoured tiny minority who managed to get to university at all in that era. Even those who were lucky enough to have scholarships were always mindful of the scrimping and saving that still had to go on at home. Nor were we prepared to see all this self-denial take place without recompense on our part. So, however much we might indulge in the lighter aspects of college life, for most of us the first priority had to be working hard to get a good degree. For me and, I suspect, many other students, the chief attraction was the well-stocked college library. The position of the main library at the very pinnacle of the college always seemed to me to be appropriately symbolic, just as the National Library of Wales on its hill overlooking the town gave the impression of being the acropolis of Welsh learning. The college library surpassed anything I had ever seen before in the range and variety of books on offer and in the long spells available for uninterrupted reading. I appreciated for the first time the inwardness of the phrase 'reading for a degree'. As to lectures and tutorials, I found that they could vary widely in quality. I am quite sure that not nearly as much emphasis was placed then as nowadays on the skills required for university teaching; much more was left to the initiative of the individual student. I have to confess that some of the academic staff were ineffective as teachers, yet gave no hint that they were in the slightest degree aware of their own shortcomings. I believe that I was more than ordinarily fortunate insofar as nearly every one of those who taught me in my main subjects was particularly good and, in some instances, really inspiring.

T. H. Parry-Williams was unequalled in the clarity with which he could expound even the most complex subjects. His radiant smile, deep resonant voice and gentle courtesy made a profound and lasting impression on me. He never began or ended a lecture without bidding us, 'Good morning, ladies and gentlemen', as though we were his honoured equals. Thomas Jones, who later succeeded 'Parri bach' as professor, was already a formidable scholar and a forceful teacher, possessed of irrepressible energy and enthusiasm. If he had a weakness, it sprang from his tendency to lecture too fast in order to get all his material in.

All the historians – Professor R. F. Treharne, Sydney Herbert, E. Jones Parry and S. H. F. Johnston – were highly accomplished lecturers. Oddly enough, I should say that Treharne was probably the least effective as a lecturer, but he more than made up for that by the skilful and inspiring way in which he conducted his tutorials and essay classes. Another historian who left his abiding mark on me was E. H. Carr, professor of international relations. He appeared in Aberystwyth only once a week but delivered a public lecture, which many students outside his department used to attend because Carr's knowledge and understanding of the tangled web of current affairs in the late 1930s was so phenomenal.

Welsh history was an independent department under the direction of Professor E. A. ('Doc') Lewis. I had the good luck to be the only student pursuing his honours course at that time and I benefited hugely from my contacts with him. Because he was afflicted with an unfortunate stammer, he was not an especially good lecturer, though that hardly mattered when our contacts with one another were on a one-to-one basis and more in the nature of conversations than lectures. He was at that time engaged on a good deal of research at the National Library of Wales, and it was he who first introduced me to the riches of that extraordinary repository of sources for the history and literature of Wales. Many of our classes were, in fact, informally conducted at the library. He was himself an economic historian by training, but that did not prevent him from having a sensitive awareness of the importance of Welsh literature as a historical source. For my undergraduate thesis, for example, he required me to write on the value for the historian of the poetry of a sixteenth-century Welsh bard, Tudur Aled.

It was 'Doc', too, who insisted that I carry on with the study of Welsh when my own enthusiasm for the subject had dwindled almost to vanishing point in my second year. The source of the trouble was that in those days the Welsh department concentrated its attention almost exclusively on the study of language. I was no *ieithgi* (language hound) – the student term of contempt for those who thought that language studies were all important – and I had always supposed that we should be far more concerned with the study of literature. Yet, extraordinary as that may seem, I never once heard Parry-Williams, that giant of Welsh literature, give a lecture on the subject; and even Gwenallt never seemed to get beyond the year 1500 and then without much spark or interest as far as I was concerned. As a result, I had become completely disenchanted and was seriously think-ing of giving up Welsh. It was 'Doc' Lewis who put the brakes on this slide to potential disaster. He insisted that if I wished to become a genuine Welsh historian I had no choice but to equip myself to deal adequately with native sources. His attitude was all the more remarkable because, being an economic historian himself, he rarely handled Welsh-language sources. But how right he was, and how often since have I had cause to bless his name for the wisdom of his advice! Sadly enough, this endearing man, of whom I was so fond and to whom I owed so much, died within a few months of my graduation and I never had the benefit of his guidance as a research supervisor.

My years in Aberystwyth fell into two distinct phases: 1937–40 and 1940–2. The years from 1937 to 1940 were a confused and sombre period in European history, overcast by the intensifying darkness of Hitlerian tyranny and the lengthening shadows of impending conflict. None of us could ignore the approach of war or feel anything but acute unease about what it might bring in its train. We all knew of the devastation it had already wrought in battle zones like Manchuria, Abyssinia or Spain. Terrifying images drawn from newspaper pictures and film reports and the horrendous predictions of films such as *The Shape of Things to Come* made us dread that civilization as we knew it might soon be swept away and us with it. Actually, for war had broken out in September 1939, it was deceptively unspectacular in its impact.

For six months or more we went through the uneasy dream-world of the 'phoney war'. College life, apart from the blackout, food rationing and other similar restrictions, went on very much as before. Hardly any students were called up and most people were left to proceed with their studies as best they might.

During the spring and summer of 1940, however, circumstances began to change catastrophically. In Europe the Germans outflanked poor Tom Jenkins's 'Maggot Line' as if it were not there, and the all-conquering panzer divisions pushed aside the French and British armies and swept to the Channel coast. The outlook appeared desperate; the straits to which we were reduced were tellingly brought home when large contingents of the British Expeditionary Force, evacuated from Dunkirk, were moved to Aberystwyth to rest and recuperate. Drained and haggard after their traumatic experiences, they gave us their unvarnished first-hand accounts of the frightening speed and firepower of the German armies and airforce. Sobered and apprehensive, we wondered what our own fate was likely to be.

There was in the college a strong and honourable strain of conscientious objection. One group of objectors – some of them close friends of mine – took the orthodox pacifist stance of refusing on religious and moral grounds to serve in the armed forces. There was another hardline left-wing element, which objected on political grounds that the war was nothing less than a capitalist conspiracy being fought for selfish ends. My sympathies lay strongly with the former group. I could not but resent the waste and inhumanity of warfare and had long cherished attitudes not very dissimilar to those of the committed pacifists. All the same, particularly since attending Carr's lectures and after the concessions made in vain by Neville Chamberlain at Munich, I had become convinced that Hitler and the Nazis could never be halted except by force. Like most of my fellow students I felt I had to screw myself up to the prospect of being called up for the army – in my case with much trepidation and no enthusiasm. Early in July 1940 I was summoned to Pontypridd to present myself for medical examination, only to be informed that I was Grade III and would not be called up for the time being. I was told that I could return to college to complete my degree but

G.W. as president of the Students' Representative Council, 1941–2.

to hold myself in readiness to be called again for medical examination and possible military service. The army doctors' verdict came as a considerable shock to me. I had not previously thought of myself as a medical risk and had even served in the ranks of the college OTC without any apparent ill effects. I went to see my own doctor, who was guarded in his comments. All he

Joint Students' Representative Council, University College of Wales, Aberystwyth and University College, London, 1941–2.

said was that I should not worry unduly; since I was unlikely to take up any job involving heavy manual work I ought to be able to lead a normal life, as I had done before.

When I returned to Aberystwyth in October 1940 the atmosphere there was unmistakably changed. Though the country had not been invaded, gloom about the possible outcome of the war was markedly more pronounced. Shortages and restrictions were much more in evidence, and the prom was daily taken up with squads of young RAF recruits being drilled and paraded. A majority of the men students had either been called up or had volunteered for the forces, though science students were mostly allowed to continue their courses, and young freshers were allowed a year or two to make a start. Women students were now more numerous than the men, and the whole college seemed shrunken and deprived of a good deal of its former vitality. Numbers were partly made good by the influx of students evacuated from the University College of London, their purple and light-blue ties and scarves contrasting with the red and green of Aberystwyth; but it has to be admitted that there was not a lot of contact between the two groups at first. In my last year, 1941–2, however, the two student unions were merged into a single body, and I was elected president of the joint

Students' Representative Council. Welding both into a single harmonious union was not an easy task and we had to work hard at it. But, from having to chair the two very different groups, I learnt much which was to stand me in good stead in later life.

Before I had even completed my degree in June 1941, I had been obliged to give serious thought as to what I should do next. I knew that I was required by the authorities to 'take up work of national importance', as the official phrase ran. At the same time I was eager to try to stay in Aberystwyth to make a start on post-graduate research if I could: all the more so when I had graduated with first-class honours in history in June 1941. But now that my undergraduate scholarships had come to an end, I knew that I could not hope to stay on without financial assist-ance. That looked to be out of the question, since postgraduate awards had been suspended for the duration of the war. How-ever, if I could get myself accepted for teacher training, I ought to be able to spend an additional year in college and in the process qualify for the work of suitable 'national importance' that I was ordered to undertake. So I applied and was successful. Once back in Aberystwyth, however, I found that I had almost no time to spare for research. The teacher training course was in itself very demanding and, added to that, were my multifarious duties as president. Worst of all, perhaps, 'Doc' Lewis dropped dead very suddenly one day on the golf course. So I was left without my mentor and without a supervisor to guide my uncertain footsteps. Professor Treharne was his customary sympathetic and encouraging self but, as he himself readily confessed, he knew little about Welsh history and even less about my chosen topic, Bishop Richard Davies. The outlook seemed bleak and unpromising, but I resolved that I would do my best to stick to the subject because it seemed to me to be the best introduction to the wider theme in which I was most interested and on which I should very much like one day to write a book, the Reformation in Wales.

Meanwhile, something which was to be more decisive than anything else in shaping the rest of my life had befallen me. Aberystwyth had long been celebrated as a 'marriage bureau'.

Many students had met there, fallen in love, and subsequently married. I was no exception. In the summer of 1941 I had met my future wife, Fay. Her home was in Cardiff and, curiously enough, I had managed to get myself a temporary job in the BBC studios there as a studio-cum-lavatory attendant and roof-spotter. The duties involved working shifts, which I found more than a little hard to get used to at first, but Fay and I nonetheless contrived to see a good deal of each other that summer. The job also brought me in personal contact for the first time with a broadcaster whose voice I knew very well – Alun Oldfield Davies, whom I found to be a man as exceptional for his charm as for his wisdom. Years later, when I was chairman of the BBC's Welsh Council, I jokingly suggested to him that perhaps we should put up a little plaque in the lavatories in Park Place, along the lines of the typical Queen Elizabeth inscription, but instead of 'Queen Elizabeth once slept here', it should read, 'The Chairman once swept here'.

The last year in Aberystwyth, 1941–2, was a weird mixture of happiness and pessimism. The happiness sprang from the hours that Fay and I spent in each other's company: long walks to Wallog via Llangorwen and Clarach, or down to Llanfarian and Pen Dinas, or hectic 'hops' on Saturday nights. I also derived much satisfaction as well as concern from my duties as president of the Union; and I got a good deal of pleasure from exercising, however inexpertly, my skills as a budding teacher. On the other hand, the rising tide of military disasters in almost all theatres of the war, which had now engulfed virtually the whole world, inevitably made us feel that we were no more than helpless children playing on the brink of a volcano. I also had irrational twinges of guilt at not having been called up for military service, even though that was not my fault. These were intensified by news which was already coming through of young men who had been good friends at school or university being killed or gravely wounded. It was typified for me by the fate of one of the earliest and closest of my friends, Arthur Kenvin. The same age, we had been born in the same street, had played together as children and had gone to the same schools. He had joined the Air Force before the war and become a rear-gunner. At the age of twenty-one he was lost in a raid over Germany. A very close college friend, R. J. Miller, who was certainly one of the ablest students of his generation, joined the parachute corps and was lost in a drop over Arnhem. These were tragedies that were to be re-enacted over and over again. For me, as for millions of others, the pain from such wounds still returns.

V

The 'County School'

In the summer of 1942 the time had come for me, albeit reluctantly, to leave Aberystwyth. I freely admit that I should have much preferred to stay there and go on with research for a postgraduate degree. I had a subject all ready in my mind: 'Bishop Richard Davies and the Reformation'. This had presented itself to me as an ideal introduction to the Protestant Reformation in Wales, the subject with which I had become more and more fascinated as an undergraduate. Davies himself was an interesting individual; he embodied in his own career many aspects of the Reformation in Europe, England and Wales, and he was a considerable figure in the development of Welsh thought and literature. I made one last desperate effort to stay on in Aberystwyth. A friend of mine in the department of agricultural economics told me that the department was looking for a young assistant. I had no formal qualifications in economics, of course, but I thought I could lose nothing by trying for the job. I was actually interviewed and even offered a post but the only wages they could manage were those paid to a lab boy of sixteen. I could not possibly have contrived to live in lodgings – not even student digs – on such a pittance, and I was not prepared to ask my parents for money which I knew perfectly well they could not afford. So it was no use my hankering any longer after research in Aber, however desirable. The authorities had made it plain to me that while I had been allowed an additional year to complete teacher training, that was all I should get. There was nothing for it now but to look for a job as a schoolteacher.

I made applications for the comparatively few jobs I saw being advertised. Fairly early on in July I was interviewed for two posts; one in Newcastle-under-Lyme and the other in Dolgellau. There was no question that the former was the better school, with superior buildings and facilities, but I did not care much for the area, which was completely strange to me and where I knew no one. I liked the school at Dolgellau much better and sensed that I would almost certainly be happier there, though I had to admit to myself that Newcastle-under-Lyme would offer better opportunities. I had been offered both these jobs but had asked for a few days to think things over. I was tending to come down in favour of Dolgellau, but while I was uneasily turning both over in my mind, my dilemma was unexpectedly resolved for me, when I was suddenly offered a post at the Merthyr Intermediate School (the 'County School'). I need hardly say that I was particularly pleased to have the opportunity of living at home. I knew it would give my parents great delight; it would be infinitely more congenial than having to live in wartime digs; it would enable me to keep up many old acquaintances – not least, I should be reasonably near my girlfriend. I also considered that it would give me a better prospect of carrying on part-time research. The then director of education for Merthyr, W. T. Owen, a Gelli-deg man by origin, was an administrator of rare ability. He was keen that I should take on the job, and I did not need much pressing. After a short and friendly interview with the chairman and members of the education committee and the headmaster, W. P Morrell, I was duly appointed to teach Welsh and a bit of history. If the truth be told, however, I had some slight misgivings about going to the County School. Faint residual traces of the years of schoolboy rivalry between 'County' and 'Castle' still lingered. I also had an unworthy suspicion that the County School was in most respects inferior to Cyfarthfa. Finally, having been educated in a boys-only secondary school myself, I was somewhat uncertain how I should make out in a mixed school of boys and girls. I need not have worried; what I discovered in a short space of time was that these fears were entirely groundless and were speedily dispelled. I was so warmly welcomed by the staff and pupils of the school I had now joined that I might well have been a former pupil and not an intruder from a rival establishment. I was soon to learn that, far from being inferior to Cyfarthfa, the County was at the very least its equal. As to finding it difficult to settle down in the atmosphere of a mixed school, it did not take long to become evident to me that a mixed school was decidedly more conducive to friendlier and more civilized behaviour, especially on the part of the boys. I was only to spend about two and a half years at the school, but I can truthfully say that they were among the happiest years of my life.

At first sight, the County School might not inspire too much confidence. Perched on a hillock a short distance above the Merthyr General Hospital, its buildings were small, old-fashioned and overcrowded for the school population it was by then intended to house. Nor did the rather ramshackle temporary buildings, irreverently known as 'the Huts', do much to ease the situation. The area around the school, in sharp contrast to the broad green acres of Cyfarthfa Park, was cramped and afforded little scope for exercise and recreation. Yet the atmosphere within the school completely belied its somewhat uninspiring premises; it was that of an unusually friendly and good-natured community.

To this, the female members of the teaching staff contributed in no small measure. My opportunities for getting to know them were somewhat limited, but even so a number of them made a highly favourable impression on me. The senior mistress, Miss Thomas, was one of whom I went in great awe. She was a small, spare lady in her late fifties or early sixties, I should think. She wore her skirts unfashionably long, just above her ankles, and her greying hair was drawn tightly into a prim Victorian bun. The daughter of the Revd John Thomas, an eminent minister of Zoar Chapel in late Victorian and Edwardian Merthyr, she carried about her much of the ascetic, Puritan flavour of her early upbringing. I am sure that I was altogether too young and frivolous to meet with her approval, but I could nevertheless admire her as an excellent example of the strict and methodical teacher of the old school. As the senior French teacher, she took the risk of putting me in charge of the newly recruited second formers.

At the outset she impressed on me the absolute necessity of getting my charges away to a good start. 'Remember,' I recall her saying, 'you can make or break them in this first year.' I never forgot her admonitions; indeed, I worked so hard to make a success of the French classes that I learned an enormous amount about the essentials of the art of teaching in consequence. At the end of the first year, when Miss Thomas paid me the less than wholehearted compliment, 'Well, you don't seem to have done them any harm at all events', I felt quite irrationally flattered.

Among the other women I remember well were Miss Gardiner, a relaxed, genial, mildly spoken and amply proportioned lady, who taught geography and got on well with her pupils and everyone else who came in contact with her. Miss MacDonald, who taught biology, was also a very amiable person. Then there was the rather terrifying Miss Knight, she of the rubicund face and very sharp tongue, who was in charge of cookery and catering, and Miss Margaret Hughes from Dowlais, tall, angular and somewhat strait-laced. Secretly, I was more than a little bit scared of her, all the more so because she taught quite a lot of junior Welsh – theoretically under my direction.

There were also a number of younger women who were easy and pleasant colleagues: Miss Nesta Jones, who taught history and was pleasant and affable to me; Miss May Treharne, who taught a miscellany of junior subjects, was a relative of Professor R. F. Treharne and also had a shock of black curly hair in common with him. Miss Megan Davies taught needlework and Miss Rhoda Thomas art; both of them were good sorts with whom I remained in occasional touch after leaving the County. Miss Thomas later married Dr Joseph Gross, a good friend of mine. The lady whom I got to know best was Miss Myra Bowen James, a young English graduate who started her career in the County at about the same time as I did. Like me, she had a taste for amateur dramatics, and jointly producing a school play with her brought us into close and enjoyable association.

The man who had the task of holding us all together and directing our efforts was our headmaster, W. P. (Bill) Morrell. He had previously taught mathematics in the school and was the son of a leading Merthyr councillor, Enoch Morrell, a man of

Scottish antecedents. Bill Morrell himself, though born in Merthyr, retained a faintly Scottish tinge to his speech; for instance, he was frequently given to using Scots dialect words like 'lassie' or 'muckle'. He was a jovial, extrovert character, much given to wearing colourful clothing and bow ties. I could not honestly say that he was the greatest of headmasters, but it would be less than just of me not to recognize how encouraging he always was to me. When, for example, he discovered that I was engaged on postgraduate research, he always took care to ask regularly about its progress and constantly urged upon me the need to persevere with it.

The male teachers' common room – at the opposite end of the school from the women's – was spartanly furnished and hardly big enough for us all to squeeze into. Yet it was a most agreeable place, and I always looked forward to the breaks at mid-morning and lunchtime. The senior master, Wilson Jones, an old bachelor in his early sixties and something of a cynic, was basically a good sort, if not inclined to exert himself overmuch. Then there was A. J. (Pop) Saunders, the physics teacher and in some ways the most remarkable individual on the staff, a character of Dickensian proportions. He was a portly, aldermanic figure, usually very jovial but on the odd occasion given to 'blowing his top'. His most striking characteristic was his fondness for using the word 'bloody'. I shall never forget him saying of one good-looking but conceited sixth-former, 'that boy thinks he's a Rudolph Val-en-bloody-tino'. Yet the remarkable thing was that if a member of the opposite sex was present, the word 'bloody' never crossed his lips! The man in charge of PE was H. S. ('Monty') Warrington, an off-beat Yorkshireman, who had a wry sense of humour and was much given to curious unconnected anecdotes about Arabs and their susceptibilities if any infidel trod on their prayer-mats.

The man whom I admired most was the Latin master, Tom Jones ('Tommy Oil'), a Welsh-speaker from Heolgerrig, who regularly spoke to me in our native tongue. Like many classicists, he was a strict disciplinarian and could at times be acid in manner. But he was a superb teacher and a man of broad cultivation, who kept up a wide range of reading. I learnt a great deal from him, more by observing how he set about his task than from anything he said to me. He and Leslie Bernstein ('Bernie'), who taught English, had the sharpest minds on the staff, and I believe that both contributed more to my intellectual and personal development than anyone else at this stage. Bernstein, a member of a very well-known family of Jewish drapers in Merthyr, was possessed of a witty tongue and a wicked sense of humour. He came into the staffroom one morning just before Christmas and vented a complaint about having been woken up the previous night by carol-singers. 'To make matters worse,' he complained in mock indignation, 'they added insult to injury by bawling out, "*Christians* awake, salute the happy morn".'

Another senior member to whom I became greatly attached was the chemistry master, Gilbert Horton, a notable games player in his youth and still an athletic figure, who was later to become a successful headmaster of the school. The French master was known as 'Taddy' – so called because as a young man he was known as 'Tadpole' or 'Taddy', being too young to be a fully fledged 'Froggy', and he was the best-dressed and most smartly groomed of all the staff. Ernie Hughes, in charge of woodwork, was a temporary master and a non-graduate; he was a most engaging man, whom I got to like enormously. However, the man to whom I was closest was a junior maths master, Elwyn Thomas, some years older than I but who had been at Cyfarthfa for part of the time that I was there. He began teaching at the County when I did, and I found him to be a staunch friend and colleague. He was an assured teacher and personality, and, by his advice and still more his example, gave me much more confidence than I should ever have had if left to myself.

A part-time teacher, who came in once or twice a week, was the well-known Merthyr musician and choral conductor, W. J. Watkins. A good-looking man, he was always well turned out and elegantly sported a rose in his buttonhole. We discovered at an early stage that, as a boy, he had known my mother's father very well. It appeared that he had accompanied my grandfather on the piano regularly and had a high opinion of him as a singer and as a man. That put us on a very good footing with one another – slightly to my mother's disgust, because she always regarded W. J. Watkins as something of an arch-enemy since he was the conductor of the Merthyr Choral Society, bitter rival of her own beloved Dowlais United Choir. The remaining member of the staff who greatly endeared himself to me was the school caretaker, Dai. (I cannot now remember what his surname was – not that anyone ever used it anyway!) He was an ex-collier and a Welsh-speaker, as my father and both my grandfathers had been, so this gave us a lot in common. He seemed to enjoy talking to me in Welsh as much as I did to him. Dai was typical of the down-to-earth, no-nonsense style of the old collier, and his comments were spiced with a salty, mischievous humour. He had an unfortunate disfiguring growth which had spread over his mouth and part of his chin. From the nickname which the pupils gave him I realized how devastatingly apt, but cruel, children can be. They called him – behind his back, of course – 'Kissproof'.

During the lunch hour at the County the particular joy of those of us who stayed in school for lunch, as most of us did, was to resort to the gymnasium and there indulge in fast and furious games of table tennis. We always played 'doubles', and the choice of partners, and the relations between them, could be very amusing. The winning pair had the privilege of staying at the table and challenging any other combination that fancied its chance. The good-natured badinage that passed between us could be as devastating as some of the forehand drives!

Looking back on my colleagues at this time, I suppose that as a group they were pretty typical of the staff of an old-style grammar school of the period. Nearly all of them were university graduates; most of them with sound second-class degrees or better. They cared about their pupils and were concerned to do their best for them, though they had no illusions that some among them needed pretty firm control applied if they were to be brought up to the mark. I could not help noticing that some of the older ladies who were, it goes without saying, unmarried – a female teacher could not keep a job and a husband at that time – were especially devoted to their profession. Their pupils often seemed to me to be like a substitute family for some of them. Nearly all the staff seemed to elicit a good response from their classes; and I was impressed by the friendly relationships which existed in general between teachers and taught.

For my part, I found the teaching hard going at first. I was young, inexperienced and nervous, and I had not much idea of how best to establish a satisfactory rapport with my classes. Some of the more mischievous lads in the fourth forms, not surprisingly perhaps, were inclined to 'take the mickey' out of me, though on the whole I had few disciplinary problems. It was not that sort of school. I soon came to realize that most children like a sense of humour in a teacher, especially if he is willing to take a joke as well as to give one. What I did appreciate early on was that if you are going to teach anything successfully you really have to master the subject beforehand. It is only when you come to try to put it over to others that you discover how much more thoroughly you have to be on top of your material. Oddly enough, it was the experience of teaching French that taught me most. My own studies of French had not taken me much beyond School Certificate level – hardly an adequate preparation for teaching the subject to others. As a result, I had to buckle down and master it as thoroughly as I could. Then, remembering what Miss Thomas had emphasized to me about how vital it was that those bright young people in form two should get away to a good start, I also gave a lot of thought to the question of how best to convey the subject to them. I came to the conclusion that first I must try to make sure it was clear in my own mind. Without that I should never be able to make it clear to those at the receiving end. I also believed that I must at all times make it interesting, to infect the youngsters if I could with my own enthusiasm for what I was teaching. To do so I was convinced that I had to be as patient and as good-humoured as I could with them. I found that one of the best ways of appealing to them was to set aside ten or fifteen minutes at the end of every lesson to play competitive games, sing songs and perform playlets and sketches in French with them. They always seemed to enjoy this greatly, but unbeknown to themselves they were in addition revising what they had learnt and committing it to memory. I found these techniques effective in the French lessons and soon extended them, where appropriate, to other subjects I taught. Looking back after many years, I readily confess that these were the groping and uncertain efforts of a new and very raw, if enthusiastic, teacher. I am sure that I committed some awful blunders at first, but as time went on things began to improve, especially as the pupils and I got to know each other better and both sides entered into the spirit of the relationship wholeheartedly. I did not have outstanding gifts as a teacher, but I am deeply grateful for those years in the County School which taught me more than anything else about the basic arts and skills required for teaching. I would not deny that in the first years of teaching one is likely to be more enthusiastic, less disillusioned and nearer the children in generation and outlook. Experience can certainly sharpen the technique, but it may conceivably make the individual more cynical and less willing to experiment with new methods and ideas.

One of the features of life in the County which gave me a good deal of pleasure was the extra-curricular activity which went on. I liked taking my turn occasionally at looking after sporting teams as they fulfilled their away fixtures. Taking part in some of the after-school society meetings and groups was also agreeable. But I think the greatest delight was to join in the end-of-term parties. I had always taken part in plays and sketches and I continued to do so. One of the 'turns' that always went down well, I remember, was a skit which I used to do to 'take off' the then very well-known South American actress, Carmen Miranda. I used to wind a school scarf around my head in imitation of the towering fruit headdress that the redoubtable Carmen wore, and the pupils roared out the choruses of her songs with tremendous zest. Producing Welsh performances for St David's Day was another aspect which gave me a lot of pleasure and also enabled me to get to know many of the children that much better. The highlight in this respect, however, was the school play which Miss Myra James and I jointly produced. It was a performance of Eden Philpotts's well-known comedy, *The Farmer's Wife*, and the members of the cast were boys and girls drawn from the upper forms.

Miss James herself was an accomplished actress and, though young, a skilled producer. We worked hard but to little effect in the early stages because the actors were painfully slow in learning their lines. Just when we were beginning to despair of ever getting it into shape, it suddenly dawned on the cast that there was very little time left before the performance and they began to respond nobly. At that point, one of the actors was taken quite ill and I was drafted in to take his place in the role of a very old man. 'Just be yourself, sir,' was the jocular adjuration I got from one of the young hopefuls taking part. The performances were held on three nights in the school hall and were surprisingly successful. *The Farmer's Wife* might have laid the foundations for a flourishing acting tradition but, alas, it was to be the only play I had the chance to produce.

In the mean time, I had not forgotten my obligations to get started on postgraduate research. I was sure that I must set aside some of my somewhat scanty leisure hours to press on with my work. Mother and Dad were very supportive and made things as convenient for me as possible. Even in the air-raid wardens' post at Pant School nearby, where I was carrying out some duties, they were very encouraging and gave me many opportunities to read. My severest handicap was that I had no research supervisor. No successor to 'Doc' Lewis had been appointed. Professor Treharne remained encouraging and put me in touch with two people whom he thought should have been able to help me; but both turned out to be quite hopeless. There was nothing for it but to make my own way to the best of my ability. The staff of the Merthyr Public Library were exceedingly helpful in borrowing books for me through the inter-library loan scheme, which was a godsend to me. It was amazing to see the extent and range of the books they were able to obtain for me. I read widely and took copious notes. I still have those notes, written in my rounded and rather boyish handwriting, but neat and clear. I am happy to say that after more than fifty years I find them still legible and useful, and I was able to incorporate much of the material into a book that I published in 1997 on the Reformation in Wales. When I first compiled these notes, I could never have guessed that I would be making use of them after such a long interval.

My biggest headache, though, was having to work on manuscripts from the sixteenth century. This entailed learning to read the rather difficult 'Secretary' handwriting in which most of them had been written. Having no one to instruct me, I had to pick up this skill for myself. It was not easy, and I can still remember all too painfully the disaster of my first experience of

71

trying to read Tudor documents in the National Library of Wales. I had asked to see a bishop's register dated 1554–65. When it arrived, the text was in Latin, was heavily abbreviated and was written – scrawled perhaps I should say – in an abominable handwriting which would have shamed any self-respecting spider. After spending a whole morning laboriously wrestling with it to little purpose, I should think I had managed to de-cipher about twenty or thirty individual words scattered here, there and everywhere on the pages. I was plunged into despair and had more or less come to the conclusion that I should never manage to read such handwriting and would be well advised to change to a different field of study where the sources were likely to be much more legible. Fortunately, Fay, my wife-to-be, was in Aberystwyth. She met me as I came out of the library, utterly crushed and feeling almost suicidal. With that fund of calm common sense she has always possessed, she talked me round. 'This is your first stab at it. Give yourself time. It will come,' she said. Her words were very comforting and they proved perfectly true. It *did* come – with time, patience and persistent slogging. I always think that learning to read old manuscripts is like learning to ride a bicycle: for some time it seems as if you will never get the hang of it; then, once you really get started, you move forward surprisingly quickly. I suppose that having to learn the hard way, by my own unaided efforts, with no one to warn me against mishaps and pitfalls, was a slow and painful process, but in the long run a valuable one. Nevertheless, I can-not help feeling that I should have saved myself endless time and trouble and gained a great deal from having a research supervisor. I know from conversations with friends and col-leagues how indebted many of them feel themselves to be to the inspiring scholars who guided their earliest faltering steps on the road to research.

Still, I felt I was progressing reasonably well in the circum-stances. At least, I had, so to speak, got my teeth into the business of research. I was sure that I liked the taste of it and did not think that I should lose my craving for it. I had reason to be grateful that, as things were turning out, it was possible for me to gain experience of holding a teaching post and undertaking research simultaneously. It was to prove an invaluable apprenticeship for the kind of occupation that would take up most of my working life.

About the end of 1944 there was a completely unexpected turn of events. Fay, who was now teaching in Gowerton, wrote to tell me that she had had it on good authority that there was likely to be a temporary assistant lectureship in history going in the University College of Swansea. I wrote to Professor Treharne asking him whether he thought I should try for it. He replied, urging me strongly to do so. I believed I should put in for it, even though it was only a temporary job. If I got it, it would at the very least give me invaluable experience and it might lead to something better.

All the same, the prospect of leaving the County School was decidedly unwelcome to me. I was extremely happy there; I was getting on well with my colleagues and my pupils; and I had a permanent job. Every time I look back to those days and those with whom I was associated, I think of them with genuine warmth. That was undoubtedly one of the happiest phases of my life. For years afterwards, whenever I saw the school or encountered one of my former colleagues or pupils, I felt a distinct pang of *hiraeth*. When the County School closed down, I must have been only one of the thousands who had passed through its portals who heard the news with profound regret. A fine old educational institution had finally served its time.

VI

Academic apprenticeship

The afternoon on which I showed up for my interview for the temporary job in Swansea was a typical late November afternoon in that ancient borough. Singleton Park, where the college was located, and the seashore that fringed it were wrapped in a damp, clinging mist which blotted out everything beyond a radius of about thirty to forty yards. I felt pessimistic about my prospects and was mentally preparing myself for disappointment. I was shown into the senior common room, where one or two inhabitants eyed me offhandedly and did not say a word. Called into the council room for interview, I presented myself with growing misgivings to the committee of four seated there. The newly appointed professor of history was an Irishman in his mid-thirties called David Quinn. He had a lean, pale, intelligent face and put his questions in a pronounced Irish accent which was not too easy to follow. He was obviously shrewd, with an unusually subtle and perceptive mind, and an unmistakably broad and detailed knowledge of his subject. His questions pressed me hard though not unfairly, but I was helped out by the sympathetic comments of the second member of the committee, Henry Lewis, the professor of Welsh, a man in his late fifties. I afterwards discovered that he was one of the most formidable figures in the college. He was determined in manner, vigorous and incisive in speech, with a long, narrow head, powerful features and piercing eyes. We took an instant liking to one another and he was to become the man who did most to help me when I was at Swansea.

The principal of the college was also present. He was Charles Edwards, FRS, a distinguished scientist, with fresh, handsome features, neatly barbered white hair, and wearing a well-tailored suit. He hardly said anything but was very courteous and pleasant. In the chair was Sir Lewis Jones, chairman of the college council and MP for Swansea West. He, too, was very elegantly turned out but with a somewhat forbidding appearance and the kind of thin, pencilled, black moustache I associated with a stage villain. Although he was affable enough, he spoke in the same abrupt authoritarian tones that he might have directed to workmen in the steelworks he used to manage. I was later to learn that this was his usual style of addressing his 'employees' – academic or otherwise.

The grilling at the hands of my interrogators was perfectly fair and reasonable, but I did not feel that I had done at all well. Possibly that was because, like many applicants, I thought of what might have been the witty and telling answers only after I had come out of the interview! I could not have performed too ineptly, though, because at least they offered me the post. That was not altogether surprising, perhaps, because with the war still on, the competition was not particularly stiff. I accepted gratefully, and David Quinn then took me off to the library, introduced me to the staff there, and showed me round. He finally told me what courses he expected me to teach. It struck me as a pretty tall order, especially since I had only about a month in which to prepare, but when he asked me if I thought I could manage, I had sense enough to know that it would be impolitic on my part to say that I could not. When, however, I got down to the task of preparing my first lecture notes I was aghast. It seemed to me at the time that even if I spent all day and half the night at it I should never come anywhere near to completing them. Not until I had struggled through the first lecture or two did it dawn on me that I was trying to cram far too much into a single lecture. It is no exaggeration to say that I was trying to pack about four or five times as much material into a single lecture as I should now. Even so, that first term was really gruelling. There was I, working all the hours God made, trying to get these lecture courses into shape and fretting all the while about how I was going to find any time to devote to my thesis.

Meanwhile, I had succeeded in finding convenient lodgings for myself in the Uplands district of Swansea, just about fifteen to twenty minutes' pleasant walking distance from the college. My landlady was Mrs Jones, elderly, talkative and somewhat bossy. But her curate son, who lived with her, was only a year or two older than I was and was very good company – friendly, intelligent and an excellent pianist. Strangely enough, Mrs Jones seemed to have very little time for him, although she had three other sons of whom she boasted inordinately, until I had had a surfeit of their amazing abilities and achievements.

When I went to Swansea in 1945, the undergraduate population of the college was very small, numbering only about 4–500, with an academic staff of about forty to fifty. I liked my students very much. In those days they were nearly all recruited from south-west Wales and were only a few years younger than I, so I had much in common with them. Classes were small, and it also happened that I knew one or two of their members very well, especially a young man called Wilfred Price who had been a close friend of mine at Aberystwyth but had been taken ill and had to leave university for some years. Wilfred turned out to be a great help because he could whisper in my ear that I was trying to pack far too much into my lectures. I dare say that I should have found out for myself that my pace was too hectic and my contents hopelessly overloaded, but it was a godsend to have so sensitive a listening post in my audience. I suppose that many university lecturers make their most egregious mistakes in timing and presentation during their first term or two, as I did.

From Mrs Jones's house in The Grove I walked every day to the university. My usual route took me through the charming little Brynmill Park with its delightful lake (Swansea's first reservoir!) and its flock of swans and multifarious ducks, then on to Singleton Park until I finally reached the college. There can be few universities anywhere with such a dramatically beautiful site as Swansea. I know of many situated in a park and some on the seashore, but Swansea is the only one I know situated in a lovely park on the seashore. Perched in the middle of the exquisite crescent-shaped sweep of Swansea Bay (which Walter Landor compared favourably with the Bay of Naples), it looks south across the Bristol Channel to the distant hills of Somerset and Devon, and eastward over Swansea Docks and the Port Talbot steelworks along the receding Glamorgan coastline. But perhaps its most piquant view is westward towards the twin breasts of Mumbles Head which figure in that old saw beloved of all Swansea people: 'If you can see Mumbles Head, it's going to rain; if you can't see it, it's already raining.' As if the seaward view were not enough, the copper king, John Henry Vivian, who first built Singleton Abbey – though no monk ever trod within its confines or hallowed its precincts – had surrounded it with a glorious park of several hundred acres. Most captivating of all were the Archery Gardens, immediately adjacent to the Abbey, which the garden-loving first Mrs Vivian planted with rhododendrons, azaleas, magnolias, camellias and other flowering shrubs and trees in eye-catching profusion. For over fifty years they have given me blissful hours of refreshment and tranquillity.

Singleton Abbey itself is an architectural pastiche; a bewildering mixture of ancient styles, whose own architect said of it, 'the general effect aimed at is Gothic rather than Tudor', and added that 'it lent the mind to days long past and possessed many principles in common with poetry and painting'. I once rather uncharitably described it as 'Strawberry Hill Jacobethan'; that was unkind, because it is a building which grows on you and of which you become exceedingly fond. The first nucleus of the university buildings, it still houses the administrative heart of the institution. When I knew it first, it and the college library, a plain but dignified functional structure, were the only permanent buildings the place boasted. The rest of the accommodation consisted of a series of temporary erections, vulgarly known as 'the sheds', which housed most of the science departments. I found it rather odd to hear from some of my colleagues in the early days that Swansea was 'the graveyard of ambition'. 'You come here full of restless, ambitious plans for the future,' they said, 'and then after a while, you find the place spreading its tentacles around you, and you don't want to leave.' That is not true of everyone, I know, not even of the majority, perhaps; but, after the best part of a lifetime spent here, I can testify it holds good for me.

Having left the warm, close-knit community of the Merthyr County School, I was somewhat concerned about how I should fit into a new and very different institution, but my academic colleagues soon made me feel very much at home. My 'boss', David Quinn, and his wife, Alison, could hardly have been kinder or more helpful. David gave me a great deal of advice without ever being in the slightest degree patronizing or officious. He also taught me an immense amount without being aware of it; what I learnt to admire most in him were the demanding standards he set himself in particular and other people by implication. My only other departmental colleague was a middle-aged lady, Marian Gibbs, who was also in her first year of university teaching. A gifted medieval historian, she was not unfriendly, but she was somewhat strained and remote in manner, and a pronounced Marxist by intellectual conviction. Relations between us were always polite but somewhat distant.

It was very different with members of the department of Welsh, in which I was also doing a limited amount of teaching. Its two members of staff, Henry Lewis and Stephen Williams, were about twenty-five to thirty years older than myself, but I became instant friends with both and remained so all their lives. Both were great leg-pullers and loved a joke, and I always felt more like a younger brother to them than a colleague. I was interested to see how forthcoming a number of the senior members of the faculty were. A majority of them used to repair to the college refectory at mid-morning for a cup of coffee and a gossip. Among the most regular of the habitués was the principal, who seemed greatly to appreciate the opportunity of talking informally to all and any of his colleagues. His one bugbear was the manageress of the refectory, who had, in a previous existence, kept a pub and was inclined at 11.15 a.m. to announce at the top of her stentorian voice, 'Time gents, all!' I used to see Charles Edwards wince perceptibly at this, but he was always too reserved to remonstrate with her. I also got to know the vice-principal, W. D. Thomas, professor of English, very well. Tall, handsome and urbane, he had been an accomplished athlete in his younger days, and I always found him easy and delightful in conversation, serious or more light-hearted. Another was Neville George, professor of geology, who was unbelievably energetic, physically and mentally, and more than ordinarily friendly and cheerful. Among those closer to my own generation were a young and brilliant economist, Victor Morgan, soon to be appointed professor of the subject, and Herbert Hill, an ancient history specialist, to whom I became exceptionally close. These and many others all helped to make me feel within a comparatively short space of time as if I belonged.

Not the least valuable contribution was that made by the ancillary members of the college staff – the secretaries, laboratory attendants, porters, waitresses, cleaners, and the like – in whom Swansea has always been unusually fortunate. The head porter then was George Smale, a man with whom it always paid to be on good terms, as I was reliably informed. A short, stocky man with somewhat saturnine features, he always carried himself with a brisk, military bearing. I enjoyed many an informative conversation with him, because he always appeared to know far more than anyone else about what went on in the place. I shall never forget him telling me in secretive, confidential tones, 'Oh! I could tell you things about this place – staff and students alike, Mr Williams – as would make every 'air on your young 'ead stand on end with 'orror.' 'I tell you what,' he went on, 'I wouldn't send a sister of mine 'ere, and that's saying something.' My young ears began to tingle expectantly, hoping to be entrusted with dark secrets of the most tantalizing nature. But no skeletons tumbled from the cupboard, not even the tiniest finger-bone. Whatever George Smale knew, he was not prepared to divulge.

It was also a godsend for me that Fay was teaching not far away at the Girls' Grammar School in Gowerton. Although we were both kept extremely busy by our teaching duties, we natur-ally contrived to see one another once or twice a week. When spring and early summer came round, we seized the oppor-tunities, as they arose, for walks and excursions down to the unspoilt Gower coastline and countryside. They proved to be the first taste of a lifetime's affection for that incomparable peninsula. As my first academic session in Swansea came to a close, hostilities in Europe ended, and, soon after, the war in the Far East also. For all the post-war tensions, a dark blanket seemed to have been lifted from our existence. At the end of the summer term I was offered the prospect of another year in the college and gladly accepted.

The new academic session, 1945–6, saw the first tentative beginnings of peacetime reconstruction. Our meagre student numbers were swollen by the first influx of returned ex-servicemen, many of whom were coming back to complete a degree they had begun some years before. They were mature, keen and responsive, splendid to teach and excellent in the influence they had on younger students who had come in straight from school. A number of youngish academic staff also returned, some from the services and others from the civil service, or other wartime posts. Some new appointments were made to cope with growing student numbers. In general there was an air of youth and optimism about the place and a feeling that possibly we all had a chance to make a fresh start in a better order of things. I remember feeling tremendously excited and encouraged by the sweeping Labour victory in the general election of 1945, which seemed to me to typify the new dawn. Like many others, I suppose, I honestly – if naïvely – felt that the 'guilty men' of Zilliacus's highly influential book had been swept away and a brighter political and social order, in Britain and the wider world, might be about to begin.

I may have been all the more buoyed up because I had moved my lodgings to Sketty, where I was now sharing rooms with an ardent left-winger, Vernon Jones, the college lecturer in physical education. A big, bluff, good-humoured fellow, he and I were soon on terms of close friendship and have always remained so. Interestingly enough, although he had been something of a Casanova when serving in the Air Force, he fell in love with one of my students, Josephine ('Josie'), a handsome girl endowed with a lovely soprano voice. It was I who introduced them and, before the year was out, they were married. Three others with whom I came into close contact because they wanted me to teach them Welsh were Jim Godwin and Wolfgang Fuchs, both mathematicians, and Ronald Shepherd, a physicist. They were

Wedding photograph, April 1946.

keen and intelligent and made surprisingly good progress. I was only sorry that Fuchs and Shepherd left after a year or two and our class broke up, though Jim maintained his interest and carried on with lessons.

As time went on, I had to give serious thought to my plans for the future. Fay and I decided that, whatever befell, we would get married in the spring of 1946. On 6 April of that year, that is exactly what we did, and it turned out to be the best day's work I ever carried out. We have been very happy since then; I will not claim that we have never had a cross word, but I will say that we have never dreamt of splitting up or parting company. Down all the years I have been immensely indebted to her for being so patient, supportive and loving. Back in 1946, apart from our marriage, events lay in the lap of the gods. We had first to make up our minds whether or not I should pursue full-time research. I had the comfort of knowing that there would be no difficulty about my obtaining a postgraduate scholarship from Aberystwyth and there had even been some tentative discussions about my proceeding to Oxford to work under Dr (later Sir) Goronwy Edwards. I was certainly keen to fill the gap in my career by pursuing research under so distinguished a scholar, although I was not entirely convinced that J.G.E., great historian though he was, was the ideal person for me to work under. Furthermore, if I were to go to Oxford I should be twenty-nine or thirty before I had finished. We came to the conclusion that I might be better advised in the first instance to try for a permanent job if something suitable turned up.

As it happened, in the early summer of 1946 two posts, both of which appealed to me, came on stream. The one was head of schools broadcasting, Wales, at the BBC in Cardiff. Having already had some experience of working in the BBC studios as a student and, more recently, of writing a number of scripts for schools broadcasts, I should have been very glad to get the post. I put in for it, but in practice I knew I had not got much hope of being successful. I had already heard that Dr A. J. Roderick was a candidate, and I had no doubt about his being older, better qualified and more experienced than myself. In fact, he was appointed. The other post, on which I was nearly as keen, was a permanent lectureship in Welsh history at Swansea. This had become vacant because Glyn Roberts, the previous holder, who had had a brilliant wartime career in the civil service, was appointed registrar at Bangor. It seemed to me that I must go all out for it and, to my intense delight, I was appointed. David Quinn, circumspect individual that he was, had given nothing away beforehand, but after I had been appointed he made it quite evident that the outcome was what he had been hoping for all along.

When this was settled, I experienced a great surge of relief and optimism. Only now did I realize fully just how worried I had previously been and how badly I wanted a job in university teaching. It is not easy these days, with so many universities in existence and such large numbers of undergraduates around, to realize how few and far between university posts were at that time and how rarely they were on offer. I knew now that I was in a profession and in an institution in which I could be truly fulfilled. I was happily married and had made a wide range of friends, inside and outside the college. University life and intellectual activity in general, and in Swansea in particular, were showing all the symptoms of revived life and purpose. I felt an overwhelming desire to make my own small contribution to the process. Clearly, much would depend on my own willingness to throw myself into teaching, scholarship, and the general life of town and gown.

The early years were crucial in several respects. The winter of 1947 was a grim and unrelenting one, with prolonged ice and snow, just about as harsh a winter as anyone could recall. The arctic weather was compounded by food rationing, electricity cuts and coal shortages. David Quinn was seriously ill for much of the time and seemed not far from death. His wife, Alison, already had two young boys and was expecting a third baby. Most of the extra academic work fell to my lot, and Fay did her best to help Alison with the domestic chores. The very memory of it makes me shudder now, but then we seemed able to summon up endless energy and determination. I threw myself enthusiastically into my teaching and my relations with the undergraduate body. On top of the usual duties I had taken on the role of staff treasurer to the Students' Union. While it meant a good deal of extra work, it also brought me into close touch with a much wider range of student officials, many of whom were ex-servicemen, and mature and attractive personalities. Among them was a large group of Polish ex-servicemen, who formed a Welsh–Polish society. One of its members once saw me at mid-morning emerging from an examination room where I had been invigilating. I must have looked really glum, because he took me for a disconsolate student and, putting a comforting arm round my shoulders, said consolingly with a strong Polish accent, 'Ah! I know. It is hard examination; you can't do; you come out quick. Yes?' I appreciated his concern, though my academic dignity had taken quite a knock by my being mistaken for a rather dim student.

Two early episodes in my life as a staff treasurer stand out especially vividly. The English Society had invited Swansea's own master-poet, Dylan Thomas, to speak to them. In due course they presented the student treasurer of the union and me with a drinks bill for an astronomical amount – about three times the total allowance allocated to the society for the whole year. Not surprisingly, we refused to pay them more than their year's allowance and remained obdurate in spite of their protests that we were insulting Wales's greatest poet. I am afraid I was in-delicate enough to suggest that this should be amended to 'Wales's greatest thirst, more like.' The other episode concerned the newly acquired Students' Union building, a large house called Maes-yr-haf on Sketty Road. For a number of the rooms we had only enough money to buy second-hand furniture, so two students and I went to auction sales and furniture dealers to acquire appropriate items, which were afterwards 'done up'. In February of that year (1947) the intercollegiate eisteddfod of the University of Wales was held in the Patti Pavilion at Swansea. Late in the afternoon of what proved to be a very successful day, heavy snow unfortunately began to fall. That prevented many visiting students from other colleges from getting home, so they had to spend the night at Maes-yr-haf, making the best of things on our makeshift furniture. Principal Edwards insisted the women must stay on the upper floor and the men on the ground floor. He also instructed us to make sure there was 'no funny business', as he put it. One of the students suggested that we organize a 'purity squad' to keep the men and women students apart! I was one of a hand-picked group who spent a moral, and highly uncomfortable, night on the stairs between the floors.

It was not only student numbers that were growing; many new lecturers had to be appointed, too. In their midst were a number of young women, which created something of a problem in the senior common room. Swansea clung to the old-fashioned notion that there ought to be separate common rooms for men and women. The women's common room was a particularly dark and poky little cubbyhole, so a move was initiated which would allow them into the larger and more comfortable men's common room. This room was valued by no one more highly than Principal Edwards, who greatly relished his regular visits there. Amicable a man as he was, however, he did not like the idea of a mixed common room one little bit. He was not alone in that regard, because the proposal to admit women carried by just one vote. The first day that Edwards came in and saw a young woman sitting in the common room, his normally benign smile froze on his face. He turned on his heel, departed without a word, and never came into the common room again. *Autres temps, autres mœurs*! It may not have been too great a sacrifice for him, because he only had a few months to remain as principal.

His successor as principal – John Scott Fulton, later Lord Fulton – was a completely different kettle of fish. Whereas Charles Edwards was a Fellow of the Royal Society and a metallurgist of the highest order, it has to be acknowledged that he was not a particularly good principal. For years the college had tended to drift languorously under his regime, being run very largely by his dominating but completely unacademic registrar, Edwin Drew. King Log was now replaced by King Stork. Fulton was a Scot and a Balliol philosophy don in his mid-forties. An energetic and ambitious live wire, he was wholly convinced of the superiority of all things Oxonian – so much so that he wanted to introduce methods intended to broaden the general education of Swansea students. Two features were especially important to him: a series of weekly lectures given by visitors as distinguished as Isaiah Berlin, as well as college staff, to be attended by all first-year students, and general essays to be read by them in groups of four. His choice of those he wanted as tutors led to bad feeling among some of those members of the staff who were omitted, but in his anxiety to show how much he cared about the scheme, Fulton took a number of tutorial groups himself every week and tried to see every first-year student at least once. His impact always seemed to me to be like the installing of a high-powered electric dynamo into an old-style boiler-house that hitherto had been chuntering gently along under the uncertain energies of steam. I have no doubt that brighter pupils responded eagerly to his projects. I heard Sir John Meurig Thomas, later master of Peterhouse and one of the really outstanding students at that time, speak in the warmest tones of the impress Fulton's ideas left on him. Rather to my surprise, I found myself recruited as a lecturer and a tutor in the ventures and was much taken up with them.

Not everyone took the treatment as well, however. Over the years, Fulton continued to set many of his colleagues' teeth on edge, and a number of very good members of the college never found it in their hearts to forgive him. I had my share of 'ups and downs' with him, not least because I was chairman of the local branch of the Association of University Teachers for some years. That was almost tantamount to being shop steward of the local trade union and was virtually guaranteed to bring its occupant into conflict with the principal from time to time. But I would say this for Fulton: he tried his utmost in some very delicate causes to do the right thing by those of his colleagues involved, and without seeking public acknowledgement for doing so, when it would have been far easier to avert his gaze and wring his hands in pretended impotence. I am also of the opinion that although he was an expert wire-puller and horse-trader, most of the wires he pulled and the horses he traded were in the best interests of the college. That he ought to have shown more tact and patience in handling people, I do not deny. But there also seems to me to be no doubt that it was he who put Swansea on the academic map and made it 'buzz', as it had seldom done before.

VII

The groves of Academe

During the late 1940s I had been pressing on with my research
and becoming more and more absorbed in it. I had read more
widely in the British and European literature of the Reformation
and, as a result, grown increasingly open-minded about it.
Whereas I had begun my explorations as a convinced Protestant
Nonconformist, I now believed that I understood the High
Anglican and the Roman Catholic points of view much better
and sympathized more readily with them even if I did not share
them. I could not any longer look upon the Reformation as an
uncomplicated, black-and-white battle of Protestant truth
against Catholic error; on the contrary, I was coming increasingly
to conceive of it as a debate about the reform of religion between
two sets of enthusiasts, who differed widely amongst themselves
and who, in spite of the fierce controversies between them and
their antagonists, had much in common. Having now read the
work of great historians of widely contrasting religious persuasions, I was deeply impressed by the sincerity of their convictions no less than the depth of their knowledge: David Knowles
no less than G. G. Coulton, or Philip Hughes as much as R. W.
Dixon. Having also cast my net into the very deep waters of
French and German historiography, I was awed by the wealth
and detail of the learning I discovered there.

I had also wrestled reasonably successfully with the intricacies
of dealing with documentary materials and was by this time
accustomed to handling them in such august temples of these

arcane mysteries as the Public Record Office, the British Museum (now British Library) or the National Library of Wales. I had been immured in them for long hours, especially during the vacations. In the absence at this time of any college research funds to assist impecunious young lecturers, Fay and I had to take our 'holidays' in London or Aberystwyth to enable us to get at our sources. Fay needed to resort there as much as I, since she was engaged on research on the history of the Quakers in Glamorgan. We began a practice, which became a regular summer routine for some years, of exchanging our home in Swansea with that of a London clergyman through the good offices of an agency known as the London Poor Clergy Holidays Fund. As a result, we ended up in some unusual locations. One of the vicarages was situated immediately opposite one of the entrances to the Tottenham Hotspurs' football ground. Originally built for a vicar's wife who was a Guinness heiress, it was constructed on a scale intended to provide her with the luxury to which she had always been accustomed. It had even had its own ballroom! Needless to say, by the time we got there, the vicar occupied only a small part of the once palatial accommodation. Going round the premises every night to see to all the locks, bolts and bars was, nevertheless, rather like securing a miniature gaol.

Without a regular supervisor for my research to whom I could turn for help and advice, I found it tough going to maintain progress on the thesis. However, by the end of 1947, I had managed to complete it. My external examiner was G. P. Jones, professor of economic history at Sheffield, although my clearest recollection of him is of a man who could tell hilarious and, sometimes, salacious stories better than most. He was also an accomplished artist who used to send us exquisite hand-painted scenes of the Lake District as Christmas cards. We got on famously in the viva voce examination and he pronounced himself satisfied with the thesis and oral examination. I then had the extraordinary experience of jumping, as it were, from the prisoner's dock to the judge's bench, when G.P. went on to conduct a viva with a lady for whose thesis I had been acting as an internal examiner. Quoth G.P. with a twinkle in his eye, 'God knows what we'd have done if I had had to fail you.'

Although I had not had an official supervisor, there were three people who had taken a considerable interest in my work. David Quinn did not know much about the history of Wales and cared little for the Reformation, but he had such an exceptionally wide and precise bibliographical knowledge and was so sensitive to the history of his native Ireland that I found conversations with him to be deeply rewarding. Henry Lewis, on the other hand, was not a technical historian, but was so well-informed about Wales, its language and literature, as to be a mine of invaluable information. Finally, there was David Williams, newly appointed professor of Welsh history at Aberystwyth. Although by the time he was officially named as my supervisor I had virtually finished the thesis, David read the text and gave me gilt-edged advice, of which I was badly in need, about style and presentation. He was one of the most meticulous and thorough scholars it was my good fortune to meet. He was also named as Fay's director of studies, but he promptly turned her over to my tender care, with the comment that there was no point in her coming to Aberystwyth for advice when she could get it all at home!

David Williams and I became very good friends; to such an extent that, a year or two later, when he realized that he was not going to be able to fulfil his promise to write a little book on Samuel Roberts, Llanbryn-mair, that he had agreed to write for the University of Wales Press, he asked me if I would take it on instead of him. Although I had only a year in which to write it, I was fired up by the prospect, partly because I was excited about writing a book, even a little one, but even more because I was so elated that a historian of David's calibre had asked me to deputize for him. David advised me to seek the help of Iorwerth Peate who, as he said, 'has virtually made S.R. and Llanbryn-mair his copyright'. I hardly knew Iorwerth Peate but had heard that he could be spiky. Nevertheless, when I approached him, no one could have been more affable or helpful, and in all my subsequent dealings with him I found him most forthcoming. The summer of 1949 was particularly hot and I still remember what a sweat it was – literally and metaphorically – to get the book out in time for St David's Day 1950. It appeared in the bilingual series published by the University of Wales Press – my first experience of a long and fruitful relationship with the press, which was subsequently to publish many of my books. This book on S.R. opened up for me not only many of the aspects of the life of nineteenth-century Wales but also the fascinating subject of emigration to the United States. It encouraged me to believe that it might be possible to keep up my research interests in the nineteenth century as well as the early modern period. Since I was teaching the whole spread of Welsh history, I thought that the wider my research the more my undergraduate teaching might benefit. Added to this, there were few people seriously engaged in university studies of Welsh history and hardly anyone else of my own age.

What it did not do, however, was to rid my mind of the continuing uneasiness I felt about writing in Welsh. Like others who were brought up in the Anglicized areas of Wales, I have to admit that writing in Welsh did not come to me naturally. I knew then, and have always known since, that I was using a language which, however hard I might try, was not wholly mine. I tend to think for much of the time in English and mentally to translate into Welsh, while the opposite process rarely if ever happens. It was made worse because the greater part of my reading and teaching took place in English. I admire enormously those Welsh people who, finding themselves in a situation not unlike mine, triumphantly overcome their difficulties. For my part, I understand all too well what Alun Llywelyn Williams, born and bred in Cardiff, and an author who wrote Welsh incomparably better than I could ever hope to do, meant when he said, 'nid wyf erioed wedi llwyddo i feistroli'r iaith Gymraeg fel cyfrwng mynegiant cwbl naturiol' (I have never succeeded in mastering the Welsh language as a completely natural medium of expression). I go on struggling to do what I can with essays and reviews in the language, but for years have never had the assurance to write a book in Welsh, as opposed to compiling a volume of essays.

My interest in Welsh studies was, however, given a 'shot in the arm' by the twice-yearly meetings of the university's Board of Celtic Studies, which oversaw the work in the field being carried on in all four colleges. The board was composed of representatives drawn from all the colleges and other leading scholarly bodies in Wales, such as the National Museum and the National Library. As the only person in Swansea engaged in teaching Welsh history, I was co-opted on to the History and Law Committee of the board at the unusually tender age of twenty-eight. This pleased me inordinately because it brought me into regular contact with all the senior figures in the subject – the 'praetorian guard' of the profession , as I privately dubbed them. They were all there: R. T. Jenkins, Thomas Richards, A. H. Dodd and Glyn Roberts from Bangor, David Williams and T. Jones Pierce from Aberystwyth, William Rees from Cardiff and J. Goronwy Edwards from London. All were at least a generation older than I, but without exception were very indulgent to the young pretender in their midst. To mix with them and other equally notable figures in language, literature and archaeology, and to participate, however insignificantly, in their discussions was as gratifying as it was enlightening. I was to spend over forty years on that board and benefited beyond measure not just from its formal proceedings but from innumerable informal contacts and conversations.

Among the very enjoyable features in the early days were the periodic meetings of Welsh historians organized under the auspices of the board. Here, one profited from listening to the pronouncements of the battle-hardened veterans. I clearly recall a lecture on Puritanism given by the incomparable Thomas Richards ('Doc Tom'), when he reminisced in an aside how Sir John Neale had been 'exiled' from London to Bangor during the Second World War. He was a great historian, Doc Tom allowed, and they had 'many interesting conversations', but, he added in his characteristic high-pitched voice and emphatic accents: 'I can tell you, it wasn't by any means one-way traffic.' He went on to expound Arminius's doctrine of 'general election', and, looking critically through his tiny, gold-rimmed spectacles at the assembled multitude, vouchsafed his opinion that we had better hope Arminius was right, 'because from the look of most of you lot, it's about your only hope of salvation'.

An early excitement which came my way was being invited by the board to prepare the text of my thesis as a book in Welsh on Bishop Richard Davies for publication by the University Press. It appeared in 1953, just in time to be dedicated to my baby daughter, Margaret Nest. It was awarded the Ellis Griffith Prize for the best scholarly book of the year in Welsh, which gave me a much-needed boost of confidence. I was all the more pleased by heart-warming notes from David Williams and R. T. Jenkins, who ended his with the exhortation, 'A daliwch ati' (And stick at it). I have no doubt that the success of the book contributed significantly to my promotion in the same year to a senior lectureship.

Not the least of the delights associated with the Board of Celtic Studies were the railway journeys to and from its meetings at Shrewsbury on the 'Heart of Wales' line from Swansea to Shrewsbury. The train spent about four hours gently meandering through some of the loveliest landscapes of mid-Wales, but it never seemed to take anything like that long, since my fellow travellers were most entertaining raconteurs, who seemed able to draw upon a bottomless well of stories and reminiscences. Among them was Ernest Hughes, formerly professor of history at Swansea. Almost blind, he was possessed of a phenomenal memory and an enviable fluency in Welsh and English. He had lectured to groups and societies all over south Wales to make the college better known and to encourage the recruitment of students. When he died, R. T. Jenkins declared that no one since the days of Owen M. Edwards had done as much as Ernest Hughes to familiarize his countrymen with the history of their own country by popular lecturing. He continued his incessant round of lecturing after his retirement, but his health was not all it might have been and I was often called upon to deputize for him. It was a chastening experience to see how people's faces fell when they realized I had come instead of him. As one chairman put it with more candour than tact, 'We'd expected to have a really masterly lecture tonight, but, alas, it's not to be', and then proceeded to introduce me as 'Mr Glanville Jones'. Curiously enough, about the same time, I had another similar experience which cut me down to size – if that is the appropriate metaphor for someone of my height! I was travelling by train from Cardiff to Port Talbot with a young electrician employed at the steelworks there who seemed very keen that I should join him as his mate. Touched by his solicitude for my welfare, I ventured to ask him whether he thought I might aspire to become a fully-fledged electrician like himself. He treated me to a searching look and then said, more in pity than indignation: 'No, mate, that takes brains.' He was probably right; I do not think I would have the practical aptitude required, and I have never felt like pushing my luck to find out. I had a timely gentle reminder that it does not pay to become over-confident in one's own capacities or expectations.

In the mean time, the pace of academic life in Swansea, as elsewhere, had been hotting up. The growth in student numbers had led to the doubling of our staff members in history between 1946 and 1954. Neville Masterman, son of the well-known Liberal leader, Charles Masterman, and someone who had taught in Hungary before the war, was a very likeable man. Walter Minchinton, a brilliant economic historian, was keen and ambitious, but not the easiest of colleagues with whom to work. David Walker was a splendid medieval historian and an equally fine person. He and his wife, Margaret, an accomplished archivist, were to become staunch lifelong friends. Last, but far from least, was Ieuan Gwynedd Jones, a former student in the department, with whom I was to share a room. He was soon to become my dearest friend and would remain so thereafter.

The influence of J. S. Fulton on college pursuits was increasing in these years and nowhere more than in the field of social and economic studies. One of his cherished ideas was that, as a contribution to post-war reconstruction, we as a college should embark on intensive study of recent and contemporary society in south Wales. A team of three was appointed to conduct pioneer research – Tom Brennan, Eddy Cooney and Harold Pollins. They collaborated with the departments of history and economics and published an admirable book on south-west Wales. Associated with them was a close colleague who was already committed to studying the industrial history of the area. He was a north Walian, Robert Owen Roberts, one of the most unaffectedly genuine Christians of my acquaintance. A member of the department of economics, he worked in partnership with a young research fellow, Philip Watkin, whose role was to inquire into the iron and steel industry. Walter Minchinton was to conduct a parallel investigation into the tinplate industry and duly published an impressive book on the subject in 1954. He also industriously collected for the college library all the records he could lay hands on from the old-style tinplate companies which were rapidly going into extinction.

Ieuan Gwynedd's appointment as a research fellow also owed much to Fulton's initiative. Fulton and David Quinn asked me to draft a paper on what might be done in the field of recent Welsh history, so I outlined a scheme for the study of Welsh society and politics between *c.* 1846 and 1950. It had seemed to me for some time that this era was being ignored, and serious examination of it was long overdue. It was greatly to David's credit that he should have discerned in Ieuan an ideal candidate for the research fellowship now being offered. Although Ieuan had undertaken no formal research in the field, David was confident that he had all the necessary attributes of intellect and interest. I concurred enthusiastically and agreed to oversee his studies and do my best to help him. It meant giving up any lingering notions I might have of continuing seriously with nineteenth-century studies, but it would be unthinkable not to give Ieuan a clear run. It turned out to be a more than ordinarily successful decision. Ieuan took to his new sphere like a duck to water, and ever since, first in Swansea and later in Aberystwyth, has proved to be one of the most gifted researchers himself, with a genius for supervising other people's studies, in the socio-political history of Victorian Wales.

The decision to withdraw from nineteenth-century history was made much easier for me because I had got to the stage when I had to make up my mind about what I should do in relation to the work I had in hand on the Welsh Church. I had reached a point where I was increasingly realizing that if I were ever properly to assess the nature and impact of the Reformation in Wales, I should have to know much more than I did about the state of the Church and religion between 1282, when authoritative ecclesiastical histories ended, and 1517, when the Reformation might be said to begin. I had already been making extensive forays into the fifteenth century, but was being increasingly torn by the thought that I must either do the job properly or give it up and limit myself to doing the best I could on the sixteenth century. It was not at all an easy decision. I was not primarily a medieval historian and would have to brace myself to become familiar with the sources and the secondary literature for the period. Furthermore, the late medieval period was even more of a Cinderella among Welsh historians than it was among historians in general. I well remember that charming man, Denys Hay, historian of the Italian Renaissance, telling me that in his experience the years from 1350 to 1500 were 'too late for most medievalists and too early for most modernists'. Certainly, as far as Wales was concerned, in spite of the gallant efforts of distinguished scholars like E. A. Lewis, William Rees and H. T. Evans, there was nothing much in the way of an 'agreed frame-work' for late medieval Wales. Possibly the main reason for this was the dire shortage of conventional historical sources. Clearly, I should have to depend heavily on the rich corpus of Welsh poetry from the period. Much of that remained unedited in original manuscripts and even that verse which had been edited was notoriously difficult to employ as a historical source. The more I mulled over the whole enterprise, the more it seemed to bristle with difficulties.

I discussed my perplexities with my three main mentors: Henry Lewis, David Quinn and David Williams. All three were reasonably encouraging but were guarded in their enthusiasm and rightly warned me that such a change of tack would certainly delay badly the appearance of any completed book. The decision was something I had ultimately to take for myself. One of David Williams's comments kept echoing in my mind: 'It's chancy; but if you don't do it, you may always have a lurking regret.' On reflection, I feel sure he was right. If I had decided against proceeding with it, I think I should always have had a feeling that I had shirked something I ought to have undertaken. I have often thought in recent years, however, with the sharp change in the climate of present-day university opinion, that I should never risk making the same choice nowadays.

During these post-war years, as the student body increased in numbers, many of those who enrolled were mature in age and a number of them became very good friends of mine. Ieuan Gwynedd was exactly the same age as I. Another very near in age was Graham Lloyd Rees, in due course to become professor of economics and vice-principal at Aberystwyth. At this time appointed a lecturer in economics at Swansea, he married Nan Lewis, a pupil of Fay's at Gowerton and mine at Swansea. Graham was to be the Elisha to my Elijah as staff treasurer of the Student's Union. Others with whom I formed close and permanent links were Tom Ridd, my first research pupil and later a lecturer at Cardiff Institute of Higher Education, Hugh Thomas, principal lecturer at Barry Training College, Dr Fred Cowley, sub-librarian at Swansea, and Dr W. S. K. Thomas, headmaster of Brecon High School. Two of whom I was especially fond were Ann Saer (née Parry) and William Greenway. The latter was the youngest of a family of three from Port Talbot, each of whom took first-class honours. Bill's first was one of the most brilliant we ever had in the department at Swansea. He went on to Cambridge and later joined the staff of the department. He died at the age of twenty-nine on the brink of what would undoubtedly have been an exceptional career. When his medical consultant confidentially gave me his pessimistic prognosis that there was no hope of a recovery for him, I have seldom experienced such a black moment of sadness.

Although the number of academics at Swansea was growing, we remained a remarkably close-knit community. The atmosphere in the senior common room was friendly and relaxed. Its senior members, who numbered in their midst some scholars of distinction, were unusually forthcoming to their junior colleagues. Ben Farrington, a great authority on Greek science, was a genial Irishman with a Cork accent beguiling enough to charm the birds off the trees, whose rigid Marxist ideas I always found it almost impossible to reconcile with his normally easy-going attitudes. The professor of philosophy, Archie Heath, acerbic of wit and tongue, was an uncommonly short man, who sported a moustache and a short forked beard, both carefully waxed at the ends. He kept them neat with the regular use of a small comb and a hand-mirror, stored in his inside pocket and frequently produced in public. A rationalist who delighted in deliberately saying outrageous things to shock the many ministerial students he had in his classes, Heath was succeeded by J. R. Jones, an intensely serious Christian and a passionate Welsh nationalist but a most likeable man. He was to die at an early age and faced a lingering death from cancer with striking fortitude. Another Christian intellectual was Erich Heller, professor of German and a refugee from middle Europe. He was an ornament to the college, but I always got the impression that he privately believed most of us to be second-rate British academics unworthy of his attention. Evan John Jones, an elderly bachelor and professor of education, was the most kindly of men even if often fussy and nervous. He revelled in telling stories in which he took centre stage (wholly unconvincingly, I fear) as a masterful and dominating character. There was one in which he claimed to have overpowered a student teacher, who had become completely hysterical and was yelling to his class at the top of his voice: 'Repeat after me: *amo*, I bloody well love, *amas*, thou bloody well lovest; *amat*, he bloody well loves, she bloody well loves, it bloody well loves.' When W. D. Thomas died, he was succeeded as professor of English by James (Jim) Kinsley, a large, corpulent Scotsman and a fine scholar, but a singularly dour and humourless man. One of his colleagues was the novelist Kingsley Amis, irreverent, witty, malicious and a devastating mimic. There began to develop in the department in real life a situation peculiarly similar to the relationship between the fictional Jim Dixon and his professor in Amis's novel, *Lucky Jim*. I murmured privately to one or two trusted colleagues that perhaps poor Kinsley ought to be known as 'Unlucky Jim'. I have heard it more than once suggested that *Lucky Jim* portrayed life in post-war Swansea, but Amis was far too accomplished an artist merely to reproduce any situation he observed. Using his lively and satirical imagination, he borrowed bits and pieces from all kinds of people, places and plots and rejigged them to meet his needs. The novel most closely based on his Swansea experiences seems to me to be *The Old Devils*, a book which perhaps I had better confess to having found rather boring.

One of the more enjoyable features of college life was the existence of the staff club, which used to hold a party regularly at the end of every term. Most people liked to attend and let their hair down in light-hearted games, sketches, charades and other forms of harmless, 'home-brewed' entertainment. The club lasted until the 1960s, when the staff body grew too large to maintain it, but it seemed to me that its demise was a distinct loss to college life. The staff club organized a cricket XI, a source of much enjoyment and innocent merriment. A story was handed down of how it played a match against the village team at Port Einon in Gower, and, when the game was over, both sides adjourned to the local hostelry, The Ship, for a convivial drink. Two of the local men were overheard conversing. 'Did you notice the secretary feller?' said the one. 'No,' replied his mate. 'You must have done; he was a very rum-looking b—r.' 'Ah! that don't signify; they was all a rum-looking lot of b—rs .' In fairness, though, some of the team were keen and useful performers. Among them was our captain, J. O. Bartley, who had played a lot of cricket in India, a somewhat eccentric Irishman but an endearing individual. Esmond Cleary was a good all-rounder, but a particularly effective fast bowler, and David Sims was a sound opening bat. Most of the rest of us, including myself, were only there to make up the numbers. When we played Christ College Brecon's First XI and were skittled out ignominiously for under twenty-five runs, each of us was ceremoniously clapped to the wicket. I felt sure I could detect a heavily ironic undertone to the seemingly decorous applause. However, when we held the annual cricket festival at which staff teams from all four colleges of the university played each other, we did not do too badly, especially if we could recruit one or two research students to stiffen our team's backbone. There was also a group of colleagues who liked watching the first-class cricket and rugby on offer at the attractively situated St Helen's ground. Sitting in the sunshine on the south-facing members' bank to watch Glamorgan play, especially on August Bank Holidays, when the visiting overseas teams came to south Wales, gave us many happy afternoons. A local notability who used to attend the cricket ground regularly and whose company I enjoyed immensely was the celebrated Welsh poet, Crwys (Revd William Williams). He was very good company and an incorrigible leg-puller.

I was busily putting down roots in the town of Swansea and its neighbourhood. I became a member of the Welsh Baptist Church of Capel Gomer and cultivated many friendships there. Its minister, R. S. Rogers, was editor of the Welsh weekly newspaper, *Seren Cymru*, and encouraged me to review frequently for it. The daily newspaper, the *Western Mail*, also ran a weekly review page, to which it invited me to contribute. I really enjoyed reviewing for the press. It provided me with a wide range of books, many of which I might never otherwise have read, and it obliged me to try to develop a concise, readable style designed to appeal to intelligent non-specialists as well as those interested in history. For over forty years I was to review for the *Western Mail* and was often glad to receive notes of acknowledgement from historians as eminent as John Neale, David Douglas, Alfred Cobban, Anthony Steel (principal of Cardiff), Veronica Wedgwood and the Morriston-born Menna Prestwich.

Not surprisingly, I found myself increasingly involved in local studies. My concern for extra-mural and adult education grew steadily. I became an active member of Wales's oldest museum and learned society, the Royal Institution of South Wales (founded in Swansea in 1835), which attracted most local historians and antiquaries. I also took evening classes in Capel Hendre, Gorseinon and Llanelli. These places all had a vigorous Welsh-speaking population and wanted classes in Welsh. Their members were typical of the working-class population there: warm and forthcoming, ready with their comments and enquiries, and not in the least nervous about differing from my point of view or putting hostile questions. Trying to teach groups of this kind, more mature in years and experienced than myself, and not by any means feeling bound to attend if they did not consider they were getting something worthwhile in return, was a helpful means of honing my methods as a teacher. The same was true of trying to deliver lectures to the many local history groups and societies in the vicinity. A talk that usually went down well was 'Folk-lore and the historian'. Reactions to it opened my eyes to the continuing survival of beliefs and superstitions that I thought had long died out. When once trying to explain to a group in rural Carmarthenshire how, in an earlier age, beliefs in charmers and magicians had been widespread, I discovered in the discussion that followed that practically everyone in the audience had either themselves resorted to a charmer in nearby Templeton, or knew of someone who had, and could assure me of his power to cure diseases in livestock as well as a variety of human ailments. I shall also never forget one elderly lady approaching me at the end of the talk and saying, 'So you believe in fairies too, that's good; so do I.'

It was a more orthodox practitioner, Dr Gwent Jones, who founded the Gower Society in 1948. Gwent, a larger-than-life character of boundless exhilaration and vigour, was the society's mainspring. Fay and I could not resist his infectious enthusiasm and became eager pioneer members of the society. It was he who took the venturesome step of founding *Gower*, the society's journal which, after fifty years, is still going strong. He roped in Mansel Thomas, a local author and grammar-school master, and myself to act as his fellow editors. I derived great pleasure as well as learning a lot from my association with them. Over the years, the Gower Society seems to me to have achieved much in heightening public awareness not only of the exceptional loveliness of this 'area of outstanding natural beauty' but also of its fragility and how easily it could be ruined by the unrestricted operations of unthinking developers.

Another memorable post-war development in which I became involved from its inception was the Glamorgan Local History Society. The prime mover in getting this history society off the ground was Sir Frederick Rees, principal of the University College at Cardiff. He was a shrewd, resourceful, far-seeing man, with a penchant for persuading other people to do what he wanted. Sensing the widespread movement in England and Wales for resurrecting local studies after the war, he exercised his diplomatic arts in interesting a number of people in his idea for a society in Glamorgan and himself lectured to audiences in a number of different parts of the county. Persuading me to do the same, he outlined the rationale underlying this tactic: 'Glamorgan is a veritable archipelago of population, and there's no one centre where you can get them to come to you, so you've got to go to them.' We also agreed that we should have to publish

The family, 1965. Fay, G.W., Huw and Margaret.

an annual volume of transactions, to encourage interest in and knowledge of the county's history, and also to assure members of the society that even if they could not get to meetings they would at least be getting something for their subscriptions. So *Morgannwg* was founded – not by a long chalk one of the earliest of Welsh county transactions, but still, with over fifty volumes to its credit now (2002), the society continues to find that Sir Frederick's notion about having to take activities to the population holds good.

The early 1950s were some of the happiest years of my life. I was in a job to which I was devoted; I lived in a town where I was thoroughly contented; I was associated with highly agreeable people among staff and students inside the college, and with others outside. My research was going well and, best of all, Fay and I were blessed with two children whom we adored. Our daughter, Margaret, was born on 31 March 1952 and even now, I remember how determined Fay was that her child must not be born on April Fool's Day – by a margin of only about five or six hours, she succeeded! There were only about twenty months between the two children, since Huw, our son, was born on 1 December 1953. It meant a good deal of extra work at first, especially for Fay, of course. A few days after she had come home from the nursing home where Huw was born, we had more than the usual difficulty with getting both children off to sleep. No sooner had we done so than the Salvation Army band took up its station right outside our window and treated us to an earful of 'Hark the herald angels sing'. This 'angelic' chorus predictably woke up the babies, and left Fay and me on either side of the fireplace, nursing a howling infant apiece and vainly trying to coax each back to sleep. We looked at one another, sad and silent. The unspoken thought that crossed our minds, we later confessed to one another, was, 'For how many weeks, months even, will this sort of thing go on?' Happily, it proved to be a 'one off'. Being so close in age, the children always played happily together when they were little and got on famously together. They have given, and still give, their mother and me endless delight. I can honestly say that we have never had any serious problems of discord or sibling rivalry with them. Even today, when both are married and have families of their own, they remain remarkably close to one another and to us.

VIII

Disturbed waters

By the mid-1950s I had come to the conclusion that, having switched the emphasis of my studies from the Tudor age to the late medieval world, if I were to bring them to a publishable state I should have to try to persuade the college to grant me a sabbatical year. This was going to be all the more necessary since I had never enjoyed the luxury of being able to devote myself to full-time research. Luckily for me, the principal of the college and the head of the department were both very enthusiastically disposed towards the idea and thought that, as long as I could find external financial backing, there would be no problems from the point of view of the college. So I applied to the Leverhulme Trust for a fellowship for the session 1956–7, which would cover the cost both of my maintenance away from home and of a part-time replacement. The trust was obligingly generous in meeting these expenses and the college gave me leave of absence for the session. Ieuan Gwynedd and my friend and former pupil, Hugh Thomas, would undertake about half of my teaching duties, and I would spend most of the session in London, part of it at the National Library of Wales, and part in travelling to ecclesiastical sites of particular interest.

The year did not begin at all well. The autumn was over-shadowed by the Suez crisis and the Soviet invasion of Hungary. International relations became extremely tense, with the real possibility that war – and an atomic war at that – might break out. Conditions were not at all conducive to study, but I had to press on as single-mindedly as I could. In London, it had been my good luck to find two elderly sisters, originally from Cardiganshire, who kept a boarding house in Gower Street and it was there I stayed during the whole time that I was in London. They provided me with a large, quiet, comfortable room on the top floor of the house. It was big enough to enable me to work there undisturbed on those occasions when, for some reason, I did not need or wish to go out. The house was, of course, within convenient walking distance of the repositories and reading rooms I haunted for most of the time: the Reading and Manuscript Rooms of the British Library (then the British Museum); the Institute of Historical Research (IHR) at Senate House, Bloomsbury; the Public Record Office (PRO), Chancery Lane; and Lambeth Palace Library. Most of my time was spent in Chancery Lane, scouring their inexhaustible treasury of sources for relevant materials. Day after day I would get there about 9.30 a.m. when it opened, slog at it until about 12.15 p.m., out for a hasty snack, then back to my historical last again until the office closed at the end of the afternoon. I tried to work most evenings as well in Gower Street.

A bonus for me was that a fellow boarder in Gower Street was none other than Dr James Conway Davies, an eminent archivist and historian, whom I had known for ten years or more. A most racy conversationalist at the breakfast table, he seemed to know most of the gossip of the academic world. It was he, for instance, who 'filled me in' on all the ongoing details of the intrigue and infighting that surrounded the highly controversial appointment to the Regius chair of history at Oxford, when the two main protagonists were A. J. P. Taylor and H. R. Trevor-Roper. Having digested Conway's academic gossip, spiced with a little gentle malice, and the Miss Evanses' bacon and egg, he and I would make our way in leisurely fashion down to the Public Record Office where Conway, having retired from his archivist's post at Durham University, was employed on a short-term contract. He was extraordinarily helpful in drawing my attention to any items likely to be of interest to me which he came across and in answering any queries I had about the Record Office and its collections.

Three others who made my stay in London much pleasanter were Alun Davies, Joel Hurstfield and Alfred Cobban. Alun, although three or four years older than I, was someone I had known well since our student days in Aberystwyth. He had recently moved to a readership in the London School of Economics (LSE) and invited me there to lunch on several occasions. He and his wife, Margaret, were also very hospitable in welcoming me to their home. Joel Hurstfield and Alfred Cobban both occupied chairs in University College, London. Joel was one of the leading experts in Tudor history and he persuaded me to come to the weekly postgraduate seminars he held in the Institute of Historical Research on Monday evenings. Its presiding figure was the recently retired Sir John Neale, a Pickwickian figure with his bald head and his sharp eyes dancing behind his spectacles. A man of tremendous knowledge and piercing mind, he was rather too overwhelming, I thought. I, and, I believe, most other members of the group much preferred it when Joel, with his eminently persuasive and tactful approach, took the chair in Neale's absence. I found these seminars extremely stimulating; a number of the postgraduate students, like Patrick Collinson, now Regius professor at Cambridge, were first-class people and have since become front-rank historians.

Another whom I would often meet at the PRO and IHR was Major Francis Jones. Brisk and martial in manner, Francis was immersed in the history and heraldry of Wales, to such an extent that he would rush out and spend every lunch hour furiously delving into those sources that interested him. We found that we had much in common and spent a great deal of time exchanging knowledge and ideas. One of the things that tickled me most about him was the way in which he oscillated between a broad Pembrokeshire farmyard dialect in Welsh and the clipped military mannerisms of an upper-class accent in English. We were to remain close friends until his death.

During the Lent term, while I was still deep in the toils of my labours in the metropolis, the chair of history at Bangor was advertised. A. H. Dodd had held it with great distinction since Sir John Lloyd's retirement in 1931. Lloyd and Dodd had been Welsh historians of the highest calibre, but I did not think that I, as a Welsh historian, had much chance of being appointed. David Quinn was keen that I should apply, but I knew perfectly well that Bangor already had an extremely capable professor of Welsh history in the person of Glyn Roberts, who had succeeded R. T. Jenkins. Glyn, in fact, told me in the strictest confidence, that Bangor was keen to appoint someone capable of giving a stimulus to American history. 'Your turn is likely to come when I go, Glan,' he added comfortingly. But I thought it could do no harm to apply, so I put in. I was interviewed in London, and, against all my expectations, was also put on the shortlist of three to be interviewed at Bangor. When I learnt that Esmond Wright of Glasgow was one of the three, I thought he had it 'in the bag'. He was an experienced and very well-qualified American historian. We had never previously met before the Bangor interview, but we hit it off extremely well. Even so, I was a bit taken aback when he confided in me that he had a problem. Before he had left Glasgow, the principal had told him that he was the fancied candidate for the vacant chair of modern history there. Esmond thought that if he were offered the Bangor chair he ought to decline it. I put it to him that there was no need to do that – why not ask them for a week or two to think it over? That was what he did but, sure enough, he was offered the chair in Glasgow. No one else was appointed in Bangor, and Dodd was invited to stay on for a year. I was not too disappointed by the outcome. Fay was not really keen to move to Bangor and I had serious doubts about going to a chair where I should be surrounded by a circle of very gifted Welsh historians, all of them considerably senior to me in age and achievement. I could not help feeling that I should be alarmingly overshadowed.

The excitement had only just begun, though. The next major event was David Quinn's acceptance of an invitation to the chair of modern history at Liverpool, which would leave the chair at Swansea vacant. I considered that I might have a slightly better chance at Swansea than Bangor. During Ernest Hughes's tenure of the chair there had been a strong tradition of encouraging Welsh history at Swansea and, even before David's appointment at Liverpool, there had been tentative exploratory discussions of the possibility of setting up a new chair of Welsh history. For all

1962 portrait.

that, I could not rate my chances highly. David made it clear to me that he would like to see Charles Mowat succeed him, and I certainly could not fault him for that. Charles, then at Chicago, had spent a year at Swansea as a Fulbright scholar; he was an attractive personality to whom we had all taken a great liking. He was an able historian with long experience and a man of integrity and principle. I was summoned to appear on a shortlist in London; but before I could do so, something had happened which reduced all thoughts of the chair to insignificance. It happened at a time when Fay chanced to be in London with me for a few days while her mother looked after our children.

My father had been seriously unwell for some years. Although I was very worried about him, I did not think his health was giving rise to life-threatening concern. He was only sixty-one years old and I should have supposed that he had some years of life still left to him. A devout and sincere Christian, he was present at a prayer meeting when, without any warning, he suffered a massive stroke and was rushed to hospital. A message reached us in London about 10.30 p.m., and we managed to board a newspaper train from Paddington to Cardiff. A taxi was taking us to Merthyr when the first faint streaks of light could be dimly discerned in the sky. I had more than once heard it said that dying people loosed their hold on life as dawn broke, and I was filled with deep foreboding. We got to the hospital only to be told that he had, indeed, died without recovering consciousness about half an hour earlier. My mother, as can be imagined, was utterly heartbroken. At his funeral we sang one of his favourite hymns, 'Gwêl uwchlaw cymylau amser' (See above the clouds of time). As I looked northwards towards the Brecon Beacons, the peaks of those mountains, so dear to him and to me, were bathed in radiant sunshine, although lower down the slopes heavy rain clouds still lingered. I shall never forget the sight; it all seemed so movingly symbolic, and I could only silently pray that he had indeed found peace and light. If ever there was a truly sincere Christian man it was he.

I was plunged into deep depression, made the more inconsolable by not having had the chance to say a word to him or even to hold his hand before he died. I abandoned any thoughts of going to London for the interview, which no longer seemed to be of any real consequence anyway. However, it appeared that the college representatives were not happy with any of the candidates they had seen and had invited Charles Mowat to come from America for interview, so they arranged for me to be seen in London at the same time. We were both asked to appear before the College Council in Swansea. I confess that I thought that my interview had gone well, but I still supposed that Charles would be chosen and was staggered when I got the nod. I was naturally elated but at the same time was sincerely sorry that Charles, a man for whom I had a profound admiration and liking, had to come second.

The next few days proved to be very tense. Not having been in college because of my father's death and my own feelings of depression, I had heard none of the gossip. It turned out that the

London committee had recommended Charles first and me second, but a number of members of the College Council who were opposed to Fulton had pressed for me. Some of my academic colleagues had concluded that I had been involved in an intrigue with Council and they made their feelings plain. Their attitude, coming at a time when I was already at the bottom of the trough emotionally, upset me beyond measure – so much so that, in all seriousness, I considered withdrawing from the appointment. The only person to whom I expressed my disillusionment was Fay, and she proved to be adamantly opposed to any idea of my resigning. She insisted – quite rightly – that my hands were perfectly clean and that I had done nothing underhand or dishonest. She was convinced that I should stay and prove by my record in the job that my appointment had not been a mistake. That is what I did, but I never felt completely easy in my mind that I was really entitled to the chair. Even now, more than forty years on, I still have residual vestiges of misgivings. Not that I blame John Fulton or David Quinn for wanting Charles Mowat; both were fully justified in thinking the way they did. One of a principal's most important duties in a small college, especially in those days when there were no such things in the University of Wales as personal chairs or readerships, was to choose the person whom he saw as the best to fill a vacant chair. It eased my mind a good deal, nevertheless, when Fulton's successor, John Parry, told me, five or six years later, that Fulton had admitted to him that he had made a mistake in opposing my appointment.

When I was appointed, it helped me very much that my departmental colleagues, though it could not have been easy for them, took the news so well and responded so generously. It was also a source of comfort to me when senior colleagues like Victor Morgan, Stephen Williams, J. R. Jones and Herbert Street, professor of botany, stood by me so staunchly. I was cheered, too when John Rees, professor of politics, showed his goodwill. John had been a member of the selection committee and had voted for Charles Mowat, but even so told me that he realized how much I was going to need support and co-operation. He was as good as his word: in the years that followed he became one of my most treasured friends and collaborators. I was greatly encouraged, too, by kind words from friends elsewhere – R. F. Treharne, David Williams and T. Jones Pierce in Aberystwyth; Glyn Roberts, R. T. Jenkins and Caerwyn Williams in Bangor; S. B. Chrimes, Henry Loyn and Ivan Roots in Cardiff; and Alun Davies and Joel Hurstfield in London.

On reflection, I believe that the initial uncertainties I felt about my appointment did me a lot of good in the long run. They certainly conferred upon me a heightened sense of responsibility and sharpened my awareness that I should need more than ever to put myself out on behalf of other people: pupils, colleagues and other students of history. I spent many hours thinking about my responsibilities as a teacher. Hitherto, I think I had been conscientious enough, but I had taught more or less instinctively without giving serious thought to the skills and techniques involved. I was now convinced that, as someone in charge of a department, it was incumbent on me intensively to mull over the best methods of teaching and tutoring. I was deeply concerned to present my material clearly and memorably. I was still more worried about how to conduct tutorials, which I have always considered to be the most difficult aspect of university teaching. Left to themselves I think that many students, perhaps most of them, would be perfectly happy for the tutor to turn tutorials into 'lecturettes' in which he/she does nearly all the talking while they sit and listen, dutifully but silently. That was not the object of the exercise. But just how did one induce the shy and reticent, the indolent and indifferent, to take their full part in the proceedings? And what was the best way of reining in the confident and talkative without reducing them to a hurt and resentful silence? I am sure that I never fully succeeded, but I honestly believe that the more consciously I thought about the nature of my role, the less unsuccessful I became.

I got an early opportunity to set out my stall in an inaugural lecture. My first inclination was to talk about some of the new approaches and conclusions embodied in my own work on the Church. I abandoned that idea at an early stage in favour of a lecture that should be an attempt at a manifesto of the kind of history I thought appropriate for teaching in a college of the University of Wales. I outlined what I believed was the need to place more emphasis on recent world and British history in the nineteenth and twentieth centuries and expressed the hope that it might be possible to give courses in American and Russian history, jointly with other departments.

I also took the opportunity to stress the significance I attached to the study of Welsh and local history. The justification for Welsh history was not that it bolstered patriotism or national consciousness. It was the sober historical fact that the Welsh had a history of their own which, despite its close links with that of other British peoples, was in marked respects different. It could not be understood as a regional fag end of the history of England. Already, we as a college had committed ourselves to interesting projects on the development of Wales in the past two hundred and fifty years, in which a number of departments had an interest. It was an exciting field which we were well placed to exploit and we ought not to neglect any opportunity of doing so. It had already brought us into close touch with those outside the college who were concerned with local history and could bring us even closer to them. They were 'amateurs' in the best sense of the word – those who did it for love. I pledged myself to give them all the help I could.

I was sure that as far as Welsh history was concerned we were on the threshold of a new opportunity at a time when new appointments were being made and more money was becoming available. Some highly talented people had already been re-cruited to the staff of the university: Gwyn Alfred Williams in Aberystwyth, J. Gwynn Williams in Bangor and Gwynedd Pierce in Cardiff. The Board of Celtic Studies was also proceeding to appoint full-time research assistants. Within two or three years of coming to the chair I had been able to make a promising start in Swansea. The first thing I did was to appoint Ieuan Gwynedd Jones, who had been in a temporary position for four years, to a permanent post. He was followed in his research lectureship by Kenneth O. Morgan, who within a short time was appointed a permanent lecturer. He afterwards became one of the best-known historians in this country, author of many memorable books, Fellow of the British Academy and principal of Aberystwyth. At this time, too, Muriel Chamberlain joined the staff.

The Department of History, Swansea, 1964. Front row: N. C. Masterman, M. E. Chamberlain, Alun Davies, P. P. Stead, G.W., P. M. Thomas, W. E. Minchinton, D. G. Walker. Second row: Bruce Waller, John Davies, R. A. Griffiths (left); I. G. Jones, K. O. Morgan (right).

She gave the department a lifetime of devoted service, ending up as professor and head of the department.

But the key appointment would be to the new chair of modern history, which was established in 1960. I hoped we should be able to find someone who was expert in modern world history but who would at the same time have a measure of sympathy for the history of Wales. There seemed to be one person who ideally filled the bill. That was Alun Davies, reader in international history at LSE, a brilliant teacher and also honorary secretary of the Royal Historical Society. He had the added advantages of being a Welsh-speaking Welshman who knew the University of Wales well, having been on the staff at Aberystwyth before going to London. We had been close friends since our undergraduate days and he was a man with whom I was certain that I could work harmoniously. But could he be persuaded to leave London? The LSE was a prestigious institution where he had happily settled; London offered infinitely greater bibliographical resources than Swansea, and the Royal Historical Society was the most influential historical body in the country. To my delight, Alun was eager to come to Swansea and would spend nearly twenty years there until his untimely death in 1980.

Some young men of exceptional promise who joined our ranks were William Greenway and Robert Rees Davies. Bill Greenway, a former student, was deep in his studies of the Statute Book of St David's and, had he lived, would have developed into a medievalist of extraordinary power. Rees, appointed to teach through the medium of the Welsh language, was one of the ablest historians I have ever encountered and is now Chichele professor at Oxford. After two years, unfortunately, I was faced with a painful personal dilemma, when Rees was invited back to a post at his *alma mater*, University College, London. Though he himself was somewhat hesitant about taking it up, Alun and I, with deep reluctance, felt we had no option but to advise him that in his own best interests he ought to accept, much as we should have liked to keep him. Luckily, we were able to replace him with another more than usually gifted young man, John Davies, later to make a great name for himself as author of *Hanes Cymru* (History of Wales), published by Penguin.

I also made an appointment of a non-academic kind which could not have turned out better. Mrs P. M. Thomas, who was the departmental secretary for over twenty years, had had a distinguished career in the WRNS during the Second World War, ending up as secretary to General Morgan, chief of staff of the Normandy landings. After her children had grown up, she came to us, first as a member of a typing 'pool' but was very soon taken on as departmental secretary. 'Ginge', as she was universally known because of her mop of magnificent auburn hair, proved to be an essential member of the team: indispensable to staff and students alike. I used to say – not altogether to the liking of one or two of my colleagues – that if the professor was away, everyone was likely to say 'Thank God!'; if a lecturer was missing, colleagues might suggest, 'we must manage as best we can without him'; but if the secretary was absent the whole department was in danger of grinding to a halt. She was very amused when I drew her attention to a comment I saw in the *Observer*: 'Lucky the man who has a wife to tell him what to do, and a secretary to do it for him.' Over all the years we worked together, I found her an absolute treasure to whom I owed an incalculable debt.

G.W. with Mrs P. M. ('Ginge') Thomas.

I was under no misapprehension during these early years, however, that, as far as I was concerned, the crucial test was going to be how my own published work would shape up. I could plan as much as I liked and hope for the future by appointing talented colleagues, but at the end of the day my reputation would stand or fall by the quality of my own contribution to scholarship. It had already been delayed by the switch of emphasis to the late medieval era. The appointment to the chair and the added responsibilities pushed it back even further. But by 1960 the book on *The Welsh Church from Conquest to Reformation* was complete. It turned out to be a much bigger book than I had anticipated; in its final form it ran to nearly a quarter of a million words. I submitted it to the University of

Wales Press Board in some trepidation, and in my more pessimistic moments I had daunting misgivings about it. I have never been, and still am not, a good judge of my own work. Fortunately, the comments received by the Press from its readers were distinctly favourable, and the director of the Press, Dr Elwyn Davies (Alun's eldest brother), and his deputy, Ieuan Williams (soon to be my greatly respected colleague in Swansea as director of extra-mural studies) were very enthusiastic about it. The volume took rather a long time to go through the press and was not published until 1962. But, when it did appear, it was a particularly handsome production, worthy of the Oxford University Press, who printed it, at its best. It not only did me proud but was, in my opinion, a great credit to the University of Wales Press.

The book was cordially received by reviewers and readers. Among those whose comments gave me special pleasure were David Williams, Idris Foster, T. Jones Pierce and Rees Davies. But there was one reviewer above all others whose verdict afforded me particular delight; for a master historian like David Knowles to have written in his review that to describe the book as 'a worthy companion to Sir J. E. Lloyd's great History of Wales certainly does not overestimate its quality' was heart-warming praise indeed. My colleague, T. J. Morgan, professor of Welsh, whom I always regarded not only as one of the wittiest but also one of the shrewdest men I knew, said something to me which heartened me beyond words, 'You ought without doubt to put the book in at once for the degree of D. Litt.' It was the first time I had ever thought of doing so, but I took T.J.'s advice gratefully and was as reassured as I was gratified to be awarded the degree. The enthusiastic reactions to *The Welsh Church* had relieved many of my misgivings about my own abilities and how I compared with other historians. It made me feel easier in my mind about my fitness to hold a chair, but it still did not entirely dispel those lurking doubts about whether or not I was entitled to occupy the *Swansea* chair.

Still, the department was shaping hopefully and the 1960s were one of its best decades. That was the Robbins era of the great post-war expansion, when there was much more money about for extra staff and new buildings, especially a major expansion to the college library and a new arts building. The staff of the history department were happy and got on well with one another. It so happened that when, in 1959, John Fulton left Swansea to go to the University of Sussex as its first vice-chancellor his successor was the historian, J. H. Parry. Parry was a former naval officer and a historian of exceptional distinction, specializing in early European voyages of discovery. Not un-expectedly, he was very well disposed towards history, histor-ians and their needs. I got on splendidly with him and found him especially favourable towards the expansion of the library. At the time, I was chairman of the library committee and was overjoyed to have Parry's all-out backing for my insistence that the library was 'the laboratory of the arts faculty' and, as such, should be in receipt of appropriate funding.

I thought John Parry was a very good principal, but I always had some doubt about how long we should manage to keep him in Swansea, not primarily because it was an open secret that he and the chairman of Council were at loggerheads with one another, but because he had told me in confidence that he was finding it increasingly difficult to maintain the balance between the demands of scholarship and of administration on his time and energy. So I was not altogether surprised when, one morning early in 1965, he came into my room and showed me a letter from Harvard University inviting him to fill its prestigious chair of oceanic history. 'What do you think I ought to do?' he asked. 'I don't see how you can refuse such an offer,' I replied, 'and what's more I don't think you ought to.' He gave a broad grin and said, 'I was hoping you'd say something like that.' I do not think for a moment that my opinion made up his mind for him. I am sure that he had already decided what to do, but felt perhaps that it might be pleasant to have confirmation from a fellow historian. Although I well understood his reasons for going to Harvard I was sorry to see him depart. After he had gone to the United States, we kept in occasional touch by correspondence, but I was never to see him again.

IX

Calls from many quarters

As well as being drawn into the activities of the Glamorgan Local History Society, I had also got caught up in another county enterprise – the *Glamorgan County History*. This ambitious six-volume project had first been launched in the early 1930s and was intended to provide Glamorgan with a large-scale county history along the same lines as Sir John Edward Lloyd's celebrated *History of Carmarthenshire* (2 vols., 1936, 1939). An impressive team of scholars, drawn mainly from the two university colleges within the county, had been mustered; but only one volume, that on *Natural History*, had been published before the Second World War broke out and put an end to all activities for the time being.

The project was not revived until the mid-1950s, when the public-spirited Lord Lieutenant of Glamorgan, Sir Cennydd Traherne, and the energetic Richard John, then clerk to the Glamorgan County Council, put their heads together to see what could be done to breathe new life into the earlier venture. Richard John was confident that he could induce the county council to put up the finance for a revived scheme, and he and the Lord Lieutenant persuaded Professor William Rees, a leading light on the committee during the 1930s, to act as general editor. In 1956 a strong and representative committee was set up, of which I was appointed honorary secretary. Professor Rees planned five volumes to complete the history, and we got to work. After this promising start, a rift unfortunately began to open up between William Rees and Richard John. Both were strong-minded individuals and neither would readily give way to the other. In 1960 William Rees made the mistake of virtually issuing an ultimatum to Richard John: either he got his way or he would resign. R.J. replied in kind: very well then, he *could* resign. Sir Cennydd and I tried our best to pour oil on the troubled waters, but to no avail. The committee then invited me to become general editor. That put me on the spot; being in the early stages of my professorship, I had no hankering to take it on. On the other hand, as a son of Glamorgan, I believed it to be an enterprise of major significance. I had always emphasized the importance of regional and local studies, and there was no part of Wales with a more colourful and interesting history than Glamorgan. I also thought that the department at Swansea should play a significant role in such a history. So I came to the conclusion that I had no choice but to agree. Fay made the decision all the easier for me by consenting to act as assistant editor. Like William Rees, I thought there should be five volumes, but I organized the enterprise differently. Whereas William had wanted to edit each volume himself, I believed the only hope of finishing it in a reasonable span of time was to farm each volume out to an individual editor. The five I selected were H. N. Savory (*Archaeology*), T. B. Pugh (*Middle Ages*), Glanmor Williams (*Early Modern Period*), A. H. John (*Modern Economic History*) and Gwyn A. Williams (*Modern Society*). I had initially hoped to get the whole series completed in about fifteen years, but in fact it took me twice that long. Like the editors of most composite histories, I found that such volumes tended to resemble wartime convoys – the progress of the whole fleet was determined by the speed of the slowest ship, and some vessels were so leisurely that they gave the impression of going backwards. We also suffered the inevitable 'casualties' en route: some contributors died, others moved out of the area and some just gave up.

These years also saw me being tied up more closely with the Board of Celtic Studies. In 1956 I became secretary of the history and law committee in succession to David Williams, the main purpose being that I should co-ordinate the efforts then being made to bring the *Bibliography of the History of Wales* up to date. The large team of contributors responded splendidly; here was one 'convoy' which really kept up to speed. In the later stages, its success owed most to Emyr Gwynne Jones and his editorial team at Bangor and Ieuan M. Williams of the University Registry for seeing the volume through the press. It appeared in 1962 and was of great benefit to all students of Welsh history.

Round about the same time, the history and law committee took up the idea of establishing a journal for Welsh history. There was already in existence the *Bulletin* of the Board of Celtic Studies, but the kind of material published in it was somewhat limited in scope, consisting in the main of texts of short original documents and notes and comments on them. There were also well-established periodicals like the *Transactions* of the Cymmro-dorion Society, *Archaeologia Cambrensis*, the *Journal* of the National Library, and county and local historical society publica-tions. But Glyn Roberts and I were convinced that it was highly desirable to encourage the publication of a journal devoted exclusively to Welsh history and publishing longer articles and reviews. The money was available, and we prepared for the inception of the journal, especially in the more hopeful and expansive climate for the subject at this time. So it was that the *Welsh History Review* came into being in 1960. For more than forty years it has been a great success, thanks mainly to the indefatig-able efforts of its editor, Kenneth Morgan, and assistant editor, Ralph Griffiths.

In 1963, as a result, I imagine, of the appearance of the book on the Welsh Church, I was appointed a member of two bodies with which I had very long and pleasurable associations: the Historic Buildings Council (Wales) (HBC) and the Royal Commission on Ancient and Historical Monuments (Wales). Both were what have become much more widely known in recent times as 'quangos'. Quangos are severely and, no doubt, rightly criticized as unelected and unaccountable bodies, providing 'jobs for the boys' and receiving large sums of public money. My own experi-ence of quangos, as instanced by both these bodies, was very different. I found them to be composed of people who worked hard and conscientiously in return for no payment except for the reimbursement of expenses. I valued my membership of them not for any financial gain, which anyway was not forthcoming, but because they brought me into contact with delightful colleagues and added prodigiously to my knowledge and experience of Welsh antiquities, buildings and topography.

The function of the Historic Buildings Council was to determine which buildings were of sufficient interest and merit, historically or architecturally, or both, to warrant being given a grant from public funds to assist with the repair and maintenance of their structures. If, after inspection and deliberation, such a grant was awarded, one of the conditions imposed on the owners of the building was that they must be prepared, after receiving help from the council, to open the premises to visits by the public. The council was a small, but quite exceptionally friendly and good-humoured body, with a distinctive *esprit de corps* unique to itself. It took its responsibilities with the utmost seriousness, without ever taking itself too seriously.

It had three chairmen during my time as a member: Sir Grismond ('Jack') Philipps, Major H. J. ('Boy') Lloyd-Johnes, and Henry, marquess of Anglesey. Men of widely different temperaments, they all had one thing in common: each was determined to fulfil his duties with total commitment. Jack Philipps was a landowner of the old school, somewhat reserved on first acquaintance but with a very good heart. When I mentioned to him H. M. Vaughan's view that the true gentleman was a landowner, preferably living on his own estates, with a direct, quasi-paternal concern for his tenants, he declared himself in full agreement with it. His successor, 'Boy' Lloyd-Johnes, was not all that different from him – one of the old school of Welsh gentry, who felt to the quick his family's loss of their Dolau Cothi estates. He was much more extrovert, however, and had a fund of stories, most of them more than mildly scandalous, about the gentry of south-west Wales, with which he used to regale us, punctuating them with outbursts of explosive, high-pitched and uncontrollable laughter. He used to drop his gs in the traditional huntin', shootin' and fishin' manner, even to the extent of pronouncin' 'Birmingham' as 'Birmin'ham'. All three chairmen were good at their job, but Henry Anglesey was unquestionably outstanding. A man of exceptional zest and *joie de vivre*, with wide-ranging aesthetic, intellectual and literary interests, long before he became chairman, he had set the tone of the council's proceedings by his incisive mind, quick wit, ready tongue and his good-humoured willingness to take account of other people's views. The owner of an exceptionally fine historic house himself, he understood only too well all that was involved in the upkeep of such a building. Other long-standing members I remember with particular affection were two from an older generation and two from my own. Colwyn Foulkes was a talented north Wales architect, lively and agile in his eighties, from whose long experience and sharp, bird-like observations we benefited hugely. J. D. K. Lloyd, suave and genial, was the very epitome of the scholar-gentleman's finest characteristics. No wonder he and John Betjeman were such bosom companions! John Eynon, head of the Welsh School of Architecture, and Owen, Earl Lloyd George, the great Ll.G.'s grandson, were both nearer my own age. Each was amiability and good humour personified, and both were remarkably knowledgeable and positive in their views.

We saw all kinds of dwellings, from the grandest houses like Tredegar Park and Penrhyn Castle (described by the exasperated Lady White as a 'bottomless pit' in its financial demands) down to quite unpretentious farmhouses. Over the years, I think the council performed a notable service by helping to preserve some of the finest treasures of the built heritage of Wales. A house that stands out very clearly in my mind is Erddig, near Wrexham. It was built for the Yorke family in the eighteenth century, and its unique feature was that its furniture, dating from the greatest period of English furniture-making, had been created for the house and never removed or fundamentally changed. When I first saw it in the mid-1960s, the house was in a pitiable condition, inhabited by the last of the family, Philip Yorke, an eccentric elderly bachelor. He was down at heel and desperately short of funds, but absolutely determined that the house must be preserved for the nation by the National Trust. He informed us that he kept three gardeners and invited us to meet them. Emerging on to the terrace, we thought that the bedraggled and overgrown gardens showed scant sign of having received any gardener's loving care. Yorke clapped his hands vigorously and called out in stentorian tones, 'Children, children!', whereupon three enormous, black-faced butcher's sheep bounded across the wilderness to him. 'My gardeners,' he announced proudly. But he won in the end; by today, the joint efforts of the National Trust, the HBC and Philip Yorke have turned the forsaken Erddig into one of the trust's showpieces, much visited and admired.

The Royal Commission on Ancient Monuments was an altogether more sedate and less forthcoming company than the HBC and, to be quite frank, its meetings were nothing like as enjoyable. However, its six-monthly sessions, concerned as they were with a wide miscellany of archaeological and historical topics, opened my eyes much more widely to the nature of the prehistorian's problems and methods and also to his characteristic interpretations of sites and landscapes. I learnt much from all members of the group, including members of the commission's staff. There were two people to whose company I was especially drawn. The one was J. Gwynn Williams, professor of Welsh history at Bangor, a friend of long standing before ever I joined the commission. At its annual summer field meetings, we spent a great deal of time in one another's company, engaged in long and exhilarating conversations on a broad range of subjects of mutual interest. Gwynn is a most likeable personality, with an engaging laid-back sense of humour which made him an ideal companion in what might otherwise have been rather tedious and over-solemn occasions.

The other whom I found particularly companionable was Peter Smith, the secretary of the commission for much of my time as a member. He was a conscientious servant of the commission, prepared to go to endless lengths to ensure that it fulfilled its mission. I always regarded his own *chef d'œuvre*, *Houses of the Welsh Countryside*, as a very model of its kind. He, too, was someone very well informed on a whole range of subjects, and particularly on contemporary political and social problems. I vividly recall our discussing with great animation the issues arising out of the Falklands dispute. We were both convinced it had been a 'damned close-run thing', from which Mrs Thatcher had been fortunate to escape without meeting disaster.

One of the most contentious topics of the 1960s was the use of the Welsh language in public affairs. Saunders Lewis's celebrated broadcast of 1962 on *Tynged yr Iaith* (The Fate of the Language) and the foundation of Cymdeithas yr Iaith (The Welsh Language Society) served dramatically to heighten concern among many Welsh-speakers to fever pitch. Sir Alec Douglas-Home's administration was moved to set up a commission to inquire into the whole question of the use of the language in law, government and administration, and to make recommendations concerning it. The chairman of the commission was one of Wales's most experienced and capable lawyers, Sir David Hughes Parry. Two others chosen to assist him were Dafydd Jones Williams, then clerk to the Merioneth County Council and later to serve as Wales's first ombudsman, and I, with D. E. Davies, a civil servant of long standing, as our secretary. David Hughes Parry was an ideal choice as chairman; he had a fine legal brain, immense experience of administration and public inquiries, and was remarkably deft and adroit in dealing with people. Dafydd Jones Williams, calm, unflappable and discreet, knew local government inside out and was thoroughly familiar with many of those from whom we had to take evidence. D. E. ('Jim') Davies, a lawyer by training and a battle-hardened civil servant, brought a wealth of knowledge and a fund of common sense to his task. Happily, all four of us got on very well together, which was just as well because in the course of the two or three years which the inquiry lasted we were thrown into one another's company for hours at a time – travelling endlessly, listening to long oral submissions from informants and discussing interminably among ourselves the points raised.

The reactions to our inquiries varied widely in different parts of Wales. In those districts which were still strongly Welsh-speaking – Caernarfonshire, say, or Cardiganshire – there was an unmistakable enthusiasm for the greater use of the language in public life and legal activities. In marked contrast to this, in those parts of Wales which had become largely Anglicized – Monmouthshire or Montgomeryshire, for example – there was uncompromising opposition in many quarters to any modification of current practices. Over most of the country there did not exist opposition to the increased use of Welsh so much as nervousness at the prospect of change. Even many of the public servants who were Welsh-speaking were inclined to express considerable doubt about whether their own command of Welsh was secure enough to conduct legal or administrative business in the language. Not a few of our informants found it difficult to believe that the Welsh language itself was sufficiently flexible and up to date to meet all the demands that might be placed upon it in the law court or the council chamber. It struck me that one of D.H.P.'s ploys with the more timorous or reluctant types he encountered was very astute. Having once discovered that his informant might be able to converse in Welsh, however hesitantly, he would proceed to discuss with him in Welsh the business in hand, in homely and clear language and in affable and encouraging manner. After, perhaps, some twenty minutes of such conversation, he would pronounce in congratulatory tones, 'There now, look how well you've managed that conversation in Welsh – without any warning or time for preparation. Think how much more effective you'd be when you knew it was coming and had already done it several times before.' This stratagem did not work with everyone, admittedly, but it did undoubtedly dismantle many people's uncertainties. Another of his more effective counter-punches to the argument that the Welsh language was not equal to the task was to point out that for years leading scientists had been publishing their findings in Welsh. Surely, he would urge, if Welsh was flexible and contemporary enough to give expression to the fast-moving and complex concepts of modern science, it was equally appropriate for law and government. I would not claim that such arguments carried conviction with all the doubting Thomases, but the genial way in which they were put as well as the arguments themselves undoubtedly helped to remove many qualms.

When we came to consider the recommendations in our report, our central convictions were, first, that we had to offer proposals that would be equally applicable in all parts of Wales. We were convinced that it would be a step in quite the wrong direction to attempt to divide Wales up into regions, each with its own linguistic provisions. That did not mean, however, that we did not expect some parts of Wales to avail themselves more readily of the freedom to make much greater use of Welsh than others. The essential point was to try to ensure that every part of the country should be able to make as much use of the language as it believed to be appropriate to its circumstances. The other consideration of cardinal importance was that we should put forward propositions that the government of the day (a Labour administration, including a number of Welsh members) would be willing to accept and put into operation. In this respect D.H.P's long experience of bargaining and wheedling was invaluable. He had kept on sounding out key figures in the government, like James Griffiths and Cledwyn Hughes, to see just how far ministers could be induced to accept changes to which some of them were anything but well disposed. Since 1967 it has often been said and written that the Welsh Language Act of that year did not go far enough and that we should have ventured much further. What the critics overlook, I fear, is how much stubborn opposition to change existed at the time and how much more supportive public opinion has become over the past thirty years. As historians should know as well as, if not better than anyone, it is easy to be wise after the event. Whatever the shortcomings and deficiencies of the Act may have been, it represented a major step forward in recognizing the place of Welsh in law and public life.

During the 1960s there were three local activities which claimed a large part of my attention. For most of the decade, I served as a justice of the peace, I became a director of a building society, and I joined the executive committee of the Swansea Festival of Music and the Arts.

Being a justice of the peace for many years was a rewarding experience for a historian, not dissimilar, on a much smaller scale, to Gibbon's experience of being a captain in the Hampshire Grenadiers and writing the history of the Roman Empire. I once heard the great Sir Lewis Namier express the view that every young historian would benefit greatly from attending regularly at a law court, writing for the newspapers and spending some time in the civil service. The first ought to teach him how to handle evidence, the second how to write concisely and readably, and the third how to flle information and retrieve it when needed. I can testify that he was right on the first two heads; but, alas, I never had any experience of the civil service and that might be why my storing and retrieving of information still leave much to be desired.

I certainly learnt an enormous amount about the law, legal process and human behaviour from the magistrates' courts, especially from observing our clerk, Arthur Uren. He was a burly man in his fifties, running to corpulence, slow and measured in speech but with quick and mischievous eyes, and an even more waspish tongue on occasions. He was an exceedingly sharp lawyer and an excellent judge of character and motivation. A leading local barrister once informed me, 'Arthur never allows his legal judgements to be affected by the foolish conclusions at which some unsuspecting magistrates are prone to arrive'; a verdict not unjust to either party! One of his more memorable asides was that delivered to a slow-witted defendant whom he was doing his best to help because the man had no lawyer, in the days before legal aid existed. 'How old are you?' asked Uren. 'Forty-two.' 'Are you married?' 'No, ' replied the man, in shocked tones. 'Well, you'll have to hurry up. You can't expect to be happy all your life.' Arthur was not often hoist on his own petard, but one day a bright young thing, aged about twenty, asked him for what she described as an 'affectation order'. 'You mean an affili-ation order,' said Arthur. Back came the retort, like a shot from a gun, 'I don't mind what you call it as long as I get my money.' I was genuinely sorry to have to leave the bench because of the increasing pressure of other duties, but was tremendously pleased a year or two later when my wife was appointed a justice. She was to serve for more than twenty years, many of them as chairman of the juvenile bench.

There were two of my fellow justices to whom I was particularly drawn. The one was a local solicitor, John Lloyd, a man of my own age, who was later to become an admirable chairman of the Swansea Bench for many years. The other was John Oliver Watkins, a deeply committed Quaker and a prom-inent city businessman. I thought he was unquestionably the ablest magistrate on the bench at that time. Consequently, I felt a deep sense of satisfaction when he asked me to become a member of the board of directors of the building society which he had founded some forty years earlier. This was the Dillwyn (later to be the Swansea) Building Society. Being thus involved, to some slight extent, in the world of business and property dealing, was a new venture for me, and it served to give me a novel slant on life in the area. The board consisted of seven or eight directors, most of them local business and professional men; I remained a member for some twenty-five years. It taught me to appreciate what efforts people were prepared to make to buy their own houses and I also learnt much about the nature of local housing stock. Both John Oliver and his son, Michael, who succeeded him as president, were determined to maintain the independence of the *local* building society in face of repeated takeover bids by some of the bigger societies. Both were convinced that the rapport between a local society and its members was more intimate and less impersonal than that which existed between one of the 'giants' and its clientele. I am sure they were right.

It was in the early 1960s, too, that I joined the executive committee of the Swansea Festival of Music and the Arts. I warmly agree with Dylan Thomas's celebrated, even hackneyed, words, 'Thank God we are a musical nation'. Having grown up in a town like Dowlais, where music was the breath of life to my own family and many others, I never remember a time when I did not delight in music – in singing especially. Although it would be idle to pretend that I myself was ever much of a musician, still less a singer, over the years I found myself listening with ever-increasing attention to the radio and to gramophone records. When the BBC's Third Programme arrived, it was a godsend to me and so many other people who lived in small towns and had few opportunities to attend major performances. As well as the great broadcast concerts, I found programmes like *Building a Record Library* or *Interpretations on Record* thrilling and educative. I doubt if I was able to buy even one in a hundred of the recordings recommended, but that was not the point. What I was doing, more often than not unbeknown to myself, was making my ears much more sensitively attuned to the nuances; I was being taught how to listen and what to listen for and what distinguished the exceptional performance from the very good. In recent years I have been just as grateful to the civilizing influence of the BBC's *Music Magazine*. For over fifty years I have been addicted to music; unless I get my daily 'fix', I begin to experience acute 'withdrawal symptoms'. I am still woefully ignorant of many of music's subtler technicalities, and would not pretend to savour its delights with that degree of knowledge I should like to possess; I think I can, nevertheless, claim to feel a genuine warmth and enthusiasm for it. Together with poetry, in Welsh and English, it gives me glimpses, at least, of the greatest peaks scaled by the human spirit.

Ever since the Swansea Festival had been inaugurated in 1948 I had been a regular attender. It is always sheer bliss to me to be in one of the large audiences present amid the pulse-quickening Brangwyn panels of Swansea's Guildhall to hear 'in the flesh' some of this country's finest orchestras and visiting ensembles from Europe perform under the batons of maestros like Montreux, Barbirolli, Dorati, Abbado or Rattle. Superb individual performers, such as Schwarzkopf, Te Kanawa, Ashkenazy, Ogdon, or our own Gwyneth Jones and Bryn Terfel, were also persuaded to come. It was an unending source of delight to me to observe the little mannerisms of some of these great artists as well as listening to the unending melodic stream which flowed from them. I shall never forget the uninhibited delight of a youthful Kyung Wha Chung, the inspired Korean violinist, throwing her arms in rapture around her brother, who had conducted her breathtaking performance of the Beethoven violin concerto and he in turn kissing her with unaffected joy. All in such startling contrast to the scene we had witnessed a week or so earlier, when a distinguished Russian conductor had bowed with grave dignity to a Russian lady pianist, who in turn had bestowed the demurest little nod of the head to him. They had performed Tchaikovsky's First Piano Concerto with immaculate fervour and under-standing, but they might have been almost complete strangers to one another. They were, in fact, husband and wife.

The other regular musical treat was the twice-annual visit to Swansea of the Welsh National Opera Company. I have always been an ecstatic aficionado of opera – a 'canary fancier', if you will. Since the end of the Second World War, I have taken such opportunity as I could to visit Covent Garden and Sadler's Wells. I remain convinced that in all that time the most consummate performance at which I have ever been present came after I had queued for five hours to get a place in the 'gods' to hear the diva of all divas in the title-role of Bellini's *Norma*. If I am to be honest, I have heard other sopranos with a purer tone than Maria Callas, but I have never had the experience, nor do I ever expect to get it again, of such an overwhelming combination of splendid voice, magnetic power of personality, sheer histrionic compulsion, and irresistible hypnotic charm. The impact on her audience might have been almost tantamount to that of an atomic bomb!

Strangely enough, its theatrical impact was very similar to that of Adolf Hitler on a young German student, Karl Heinz Spalt, better known in after years as Professor Keith Spalding, professor of German at Bangor. When Keith was my colleague in Swansea I remember him describing the impression made on him by Hitler in 1934, later recounted graphically in his book, *The Long March*. Keith hated Hitler and all he stood for, but could not help observing the overpowering theatrical effect he had on his audience.

The interesting feature of the Welsh National Opera Company over the last half-century has been its growing professionalism, and the prestige and reputation that have deservedly sprung up around it. The steadily widening range and diversity of its repertoire have been no less impressive. It has long since emerged as one of the more talented European operatic companies, whose new productions are eagerly welcomed not only in this country but abroad as well. Nothing about it evokes more enthusiasm than the bright, disciplined warmth and brio of its Welsh chorus. That is as it should be, because if there is anything that the Welsh have executed with above-average zest and gusto it is choral singing.

The national talent for choral singing used to be exhibited very strikingly, although on a reduced scale, in the memorable annual performances of the Neath Opera Company. They used to take over the Craig-y-nos theatre in the Swansea Valley for two or three weeks every summer, in order to put on a new production each year. Although their principals were professional operatic singers, their chorus was made up of members of the society, who sang with uninhibited *hwyl* and vitality. Craig-y-nos had been the immortal Adelina Patti's former home, built by that incomparable diva at astronomical cost, and containing within it the most charming *bijou* theatre where she entertained her guests. Set in a delightful park, it offered a magical summer's evening out, and was often not unjustly hailed as 'the Welsh Glyndebourne'. For years on end we were confirmed habitués of the place.

I am not unaware, that in opera, as in every stage production, things can, on occasion, go hopelessly awry. Puccini's *Tosca* is an opera of which I am intensely fond, in spite of all the criticisms that are levied of its being vulgar, sentimental and melodramatic. It ends with the heartbroken heroine, in her despair, plunging over the battlements of Sant Angelo to her doom in the river Tiber below. One unforgettable evening, our Tosca, Kyra Vane, duly leapt to where the murky waters of the Tiber should have closed over her. Alas! the trampoline on which she was scheduled to jump had been placed too high, and the tragic Kyra bounced back up again in full sight of her audience from the waist upwards. She took it all with uncommonly good humour and earned herself a louder burst of applause for the gallant and jocular manner in which she accepted her mischance than she would have done if everything had gone to plan. What would one not give to be thus able always to bounce back from meeting calamity with such unflurried poise!

X

The broadcasting arena

In the early summer of 1965 it gave me intense satisfaction to be invited by the government to become chairman of the Broadcasting Council for Wales and a governor of the BBC. I had long been interested in broadcasting and had done quite a bit of it myself. I was well acquainted with some of the leading figures in Welsh broadcasting and looked forward with eagerness, not unmixed with a certain twinge of nervousness, to working with them. I realized from the beginning that this would be very much a job of two parts: the one carrying a weight of responsibility in Wales and the other an even greater burden in London. If it was important to interpret London to Wales, it was likely to be still more vital to try to make sure that Welsh interests were adequately represented to London.

My tenure of the chairmanship was dealt a devastating blow at the outset by the sudden death, at the height of his powers, of Hywel Davies, Wales's outstanding broadcaster. It could not have come at a worse time for Wales. We had lost not only a brilliant performer but also our head of programmes, a man brimming over with ideas and practical experience. This at the point when Wales was looking forward to its very own broadcasting service for the first time and when Hywel was most needed. Worst of all, Alun Oldfield Davies, head of the BBC in Wales, was on the point of retiring after many years of distinguished service, and his heir apparent, as was widely recognized in broadcasting circles, outside Wales no less than inside, was indisputably Hywel Davies. It

Princess Margaret and G.W. at the opening of the BBC headquarters, Llandaff, 1967.

came as all the more of a personal blow for me because I had known Hywel well for many years and had been counting on having his help and guidance. It was a very sad moment when the first official function I had to perform as chairman of the Broadcasting Council was to pay tribute to him at his funeral service in September 1965. The BBC was left with no alternative but to ask Alun Oldfield to carry on as controller for Wales for the time being. He, sterling character that he was, agreed to do so even though his own health was far from good. The BBC's director-general, Hugh Greene, summed up the position well when he commented, 'We must never again put all our eggs in one basket, however inevitable that basket may look to us to be.'

For two years it was a privilege and a delight for me to be closely associated with Alun Oldfield Davies. He was controller from 1945 to 1967 and, during that time, he bestrode the Welsh region like a colossus, literally and metaphorically. It gave everyone connected with broadcasting incredible satisfaction that the crowning event of his career should have been the opening of the new headquarters for Wales at Llandaff on St David's Day 1967. This was the building which Alun Oldfield had done more than any other individual to plan and to bring to fruition. It was formally opened on an idyllic spring day by HRH Princess Margaret. She was in splendid form – charming, out-going and good-humoured in spite of her personal problems at the time. She amused everyone when she declared, on learning that the former BBC studios in Park Place were to be used for adult education, 'I'm all for adult education. It's excellent for the likes of me who had to leave school early.' All the BBC's 'top brass' were present – as much to show their respect for the retiring controller, as for the new premises. Hugh Greene told me on that occasion that the new building was unquestionably the best the BBC had outside London. Thirty-five years on, however, it is out- dated and far too cramped; the problem of what to do about new accommodation is now causing severe headaches.

I was never associated with anyone whom I admired and respected more than Alun Oldfield. Presenting him for the honorary degree of Ll D of the University of Wales, I described him as 'rational and humane, but not soft or spineless; patriotic and principled, yet neither bigoted nor myopic; assured without being assertive, adroit but not devious'. He had made a unique and unsurpassed contribution to the development of Welsh broadcasting, and one unlikely ever to be equalled. But how did we find an adequate successor for one whose character out-matched even his talents?

Over the year or two following Hywel's death the difficulty of the task was made abundantly and painfully clear. People in London were no less anxious to find a successor than we were in Wales, but it did not appear to them to be necessary to find an acceptable Welshman; all that mattered was to produce someone who understood broadcasting and who would, at least, be not unsympathetic to Wales. I saw things differently and so, I knew, would the Broadcasting Council of Wales and many of my compatriots. They were as well aware as I was that the head of broadcasting in Wales was a figure critical to the whole of Welsh life and culture – not least because Alun Oldfield Davies had made it so. It was essential, therefore, to appoint someone who understood and cared for the specifics of Welsh life. The trouble was that there was no one in Welsh broadcasting at the time who could be recommended; such was the dearth that senior figures in London and Wales were suggesting my name. Gratifying though that was, I dismissed the idea out of hand, being convinced, first, that I did not want to leave university life and, second, that, even if I did, a professional broadcaster was needed. A number of potential candidates were mooted by London, and I met and talked with some of them. Agreeable men though they were, and eminently suitable for some senior posts no doubt, I knew in my bones that they would not do for Wales.

In the end, it was John Arkell, head of administration in London, who offered us an unexpected way out of our predicament. He had in his department a Welshman who was controller of finance and whom he thought could be induced to come back to Wales. I met John Rowley, the man in question, and took an immediate liking to him, but he himself had serious doubts. Not only did he have a promising career ahead of him in London, but even more worrying was that, although an excellent administrator, he had only limited personal experience as a broadcaster. He was, however, persuaded that he owed it to Wales to return and, for several years, made a very good controller. He was a man of outstanding administrative skills and had considerable qualities as a diplomat, which he used to advantage. It is true that he always lacked the instinctive awareness of the natural broadcaster, and he himself was conscious of that. That was where the BBC in Wales could have done with Hywel Davies's genius during those pioneering years. On the other hand, John Rowley was always willing to take advice from gifted programme people like Aneirin Talfan Davies or D. J. Thomas, and proved to be a sound judge of opinions presented to him.

My own impression was that the staff of BBC Wales were responding well to the challenge of these years. Sound broadcasting, in Welsh and English, which had a long and successful background, was continuing to build on its earlier foundations. Those engaged in radio broadcasting, however, could hardly avoid a growing suspicion that their position was being over-shadowed by the immense and growing popularity of television. For my part, I was convinced that there was a considerable future for the new local radio stations which the BBC was pro-posing to set up. It became obvious that Swansea was the one place in Wales which had any chance of getting such a station. I tried very hard, but unavailingly as it turned out, to secure the establishment of a local radio station at Swansea in the studios closed down there as a result of the opening of the new head-quarters at Llandaff. Broadcasting figures in Swansea and district, like my friend Ifor Thomas, the blind doctor, who led the protest, were dead set against the proposal, on the grounds that they wanted a 'proper' radio station not a 'feeble imitation'. All I think they succeeded in doing was to ruin the prospects of a BBC local radio station, leaving the field clear for the commercial Swansea Sound, which was to prove what an excellent centre Swansea was for the purpose of area broadcasting.

The staff on the television side of BBC Wales, although buoyed up by the prospects of working in a service which was capturing more and more of the attention of the public, had a steep hill to climb. Welsh-language television found it especially hard going in the realm of drama and light entertainment, where it was at a marked disadvantage. It was obliged to compete with the BBC's other channels as well as ITV, which could draw upon the resources of a professional entertainment industry operating through the commercial theatre, music halls, clubs and the like, which hardly existed at all in a Welsh-language context. Nor had Welsh programme-makers anything like the financial resources which their rivals enjoyed. All credit to the broadcasters of those years in Wales, who were exerting themselves to create pro-gramme schedules almost from scratch and, in the process, experimenting bravely. Inevitably, in such circumstances, neither the writers nor the performers always 'rang the bell'. We always encouraged members of the Broadcasting Council to watch the newer and often more controversial programmes and give their candid opinions on them. On the whole, the council proved to be an invaluable sounding board, but there were occasions when its views could lead to complications, much the most awkward of which arose in connection with the experimental series called *Stiwdio B*. In retrospect, it is surprising to remember that the programme's most promising performers were Ryan and Ronnie. *Stiwdio B* went in a good deal for satire and took among its targets some of the sacred cows of Welsh life, especially the Gorsedd and the Eisteddfod. Admittedly, its handling of such subjects was less than deft, but I think the real trouble arose because some members of the council were not accustomed to satire and were incensed by *Stiwdio B*'s irreverent attitudes. There ensued indignant demands that the council should insist upon the instant withdrawal of the programme. Happily, wiser counsels prevailed. The critics were brought to recognize that it would be disastrous for the best interests of broadcasting if the council should come to be regarded as a body issuing edicts to broadcasting staff, forbidding programmes it did not like; even worse that they should be seen as a group of old fogies bent on exorcizing criticism it regarded as 'seditious'. Nevertheless, the discussions were not without their value, if only for reminding all parties that one of the fundamental issues for broadcasters is that the claim to freedom of expression brings with it a corresponding awareness of responsibility.

Overall, I immensely enjoyed my relationship with the Broadcasting Council for Wales and warmly appreciated its role in guiding the BBC's activities. A group of about a dozen men and women, it was always chosen by representatives of the BBC's Advisory Council with the greatest care so as to try to ensure that it was a representative cross-section of all aspects of Welsh life. Its members served for a term of four years, and this practice of rotation provided a valuable blend of continuity and change. Each meeting of the council was attended by the senior broadcasting staff, and members of council were offered the opportunity of freely speaking their minds and asking questions about any subject concerning broadcasting, of which they normally took full advantage. I was always impressed by the keen interest members took and the constructive suggestions they offered. There was, it has to be admitted, a certain amount of tension from time to time between those who were Welsh-speaking and those who were not, but it was, in general, a creative tension in which each side genuinely sought to understand and, as far as it could, accommodate the other's point of view. On occasion, I found it something of a delicate balancing act trying to make sure that both groups got a fair deal, but the abiding impression made on me was how conscientiously members sought to fulfil their role. In an effort to improve communications between the council and the public, it had long been the practice to hold a number of meetings outside Cardiff at appropriate centres in all parts of Wales. This gave us the chance to invite representatives of local government and the public to lunch, so giving them the opportunity of airing their views.

The late 1960s were not the easiest of times for the BBC in Wales. Being the land of hills and mountains that it is, Wales presents serious problems of television reception. There were relatively wide areas which either could not get BBC television at all or could only receive it very poorly. The questions most frequently put to the council in its meetings outside Cardiff were those relating to the quality of reception. Licence-payers expect to be supplied with good-quality television, no matter what the problems, and are not readily pacified! These years also saw the growing influence of agitation by the Welsh Language Society and other bodies on behalf of the language. Representatives of the society asked on more than one occasion to be allowed to send a deputation to meet the council. When they arrived, they were invited to address the meeting in Welsh. In the absence of instant translation facilities it was agreed that I should act as interpreter and translate from Welsh to English. Such translation created some difficulty over the time lag involved, but we thought it was important it should be undertaken, partly as a vindication of the recently introduced principle of 'equal validity' for both languages, and partly because it created a better atmosphere, we hoped. Although, from time to time, wilder statements on the part of language enthusiasts were reported in the press and elsewhere about the justification for using what was described as 'controlled' or 'symbolic' violence and Broadcasting House in Llandaff had to be evacuated on account of a bomb scare, all the discussions we had with the society were civilized and reasonable, even if we could not by any means grant them everything they wanted.

The most controversial issues, however, emerged in the run-up to, and including, the investiture of the Prince of Wales. The BBC clearly had a central role to fulfil in broadcasting the ceremony to a worldwide audience estimated to number about 500 millions. The monarchy, and especially Prince Charles himself, were decidedly more popular then than they are now. Even in the late 1960s, however, there was a substantial minority in Wales hotly opposed to the whole notion of an investiture and it gave vent to its feelings in no uncertain manner. Such outbursts were, inevitably, reported, and the issues discussed on air. This was not at all to the liking of the secretary of state for Wales, George Thomas, who was already in bad odour with the Welsh Language Society and Plaid Cymru. I had previously got on quite well with George, but I now found myself being summoned to the secretarial presence and subjected to a furious dressing down for my misdemeanours. The secretary of state gave it as his opinion that the BBC in Wales had been 'taken over by Welsh Nationalists' and told me emphatically that 'all this anti-monarchist propaganda must stop'. My attempts to explain that I had no power to stop the BBC from reporting newsworthy items, and that even if I had I would not use it, seemed only to infuriate him all the more. 'I'll tell the prime minister about you,' he yelled hysterically. He appeared to me to be hell-bent on making the investiture a massive personal triumph for himself with which nothing must be allowed to interfere. What I did not know until thirty years later, when the relevant Cabinet papers were made public for the first time, was that he was actually writing confidential letters to the prime minister to express his grave concern about the effect that Welsh Nationalists were allegedly having on Prince Charles. It may be, in fact, that all the criticisms and satire – some of it in distinctly poor taste – directed at the investiture to some extent badly backfired. I know, for instance, that Dr Gwynfor Evans, then president of Plaid Cymru and the party's first member of Parliament, believed that excessive attacks on the monarchy and Prince Charles may have been an important factor in causing him to lose his seat in Carmarthen at the next election. On the other hand, the BBC in London might have shown more readiness to make it a distinctly Welsh occasion. For example, one of the central features was a face-to-face interview with the Prince of Wales, but all my efforts to get Huw Wheldon and not Cliff Michelmore as the interviewer went for naught.

Looking back at my years with the BBC in Wales it still seems to me that I saw it at its best at the time of the Aberfan disaster. On that fateful morning when the tip slid down on its engulfing course, the Broadcasting Council was meeting in Dolgellau. Cardiff staff rang through to inform Alun Oldfield and Aneirin Talfan, but at first no one realized the horrendous scale of the disaster. During the next few days we were left with no illusions about how catastrophic an event it had been. While broadcasters could not do much to mitigate the horror, they could at least report up-to-the minute news, broadcast urgent messages and appeals, and give surviving victims, relatives and eyewitnesses the opportunity to tell their stories and vent their feelings. In common with many others, broadcasters worked like Trojans around the clock. It seemed to me to be only fair to let them all know how proud the Broadcasting Council was of their endeavours in the course of this overwhelming national tragedy, and I sent a letter to each member of staff accordingly.

One other episode in the outcome of which I could take some modest satisfaction was in the saving of the BBC's Welsh Orchestra. In 1969 economies being proposed centrally seriously threatened the continued existence of that orchestra. It would, of course, be absurd to try to claim that I saved it single-handedly, but I did provide a rallying point for its defenders. At that time it was not much more than a chamber orchestra, but it was to prove a core capable of great subsequent development. Since then it has become one of Wales's most treasured cultural adornments. Although I cannot take any credit for its subsequent expansion, I do feel a huge sense of pride in its achievement.

The wrangle over the orchestra was not a bad example of the nature of the relationship existing between London and Wales. In my experience, it was not so much that London wanted to dominate Wales and the other regions, but that it frequently did not seem to be aware of what really mattered to them. It was hardly surprising in view of the vast amount of business being transacted in London when the BBC dominated broadcasting in a way it has long since ceased to do. So it meant that the concerns of Wales had constantly and effectively to be brought to London's notice. It would be silly to contend that they were, as a result, always decided and implemented in Wales's favour, but they were normally given a fair and attentive hearing. That was all the more impressive because the corporation was undergoing a vast expansion of all its activities in the mid-1960s. It was the aftermath of the Pilkington Report, which had been very favourable to the BBC. This was the time when BBC2 was establishing itself quickly as a popular channel, and when colour television would soon be introduced. Many talented people were given their heads in these years, among them some of the most gifted individuals with whom I ever had the good fortune to be associated: David Attenborough, Paul Fox, Alastair Milne and others like them.

Success and harmony ultimately depended on good working relations between the chairman and his board of governors on the one hand, and the director-general and his senior staff who formed the board of management on the other. The governors spoke – in theory at least – as the voice of public opinion, although quite how you were ever able coherently to present the diverse and amorphous views of fifty millions of the great British public I never really understood, and the board of management represented the broadcasters. In one form or another, the same central issue kept on coming up time and again: how, in a free society, did you give broadcasters independence and freedom without allowing them to exceed the bounds of responsibility and answerability? One example of this which still lies on my conscience was the question of whether or not to broadcast Peter Watkins's *The War Game*, a television play which sought to depict in the most realistic terms the condition of society after an outbreak of atomic war. The issue at stake was, would it give rise to excessive public alarm? Quite exceptionally, the programme was privately shown to the governors beforehand to ascertain their opinions. Nearly all those who saw it decided that it was likely to give rise to widespread panic, especially perhaps among the elderly and those of a nervous disposition. I demurred from this view, but much more limply than I think I ought to have done. The programme was subsequently widely exhibited in clubs, film societies and the like without calamitous ill effects. I still feel guilty that I did not express my opinion more forcefully and dissociate myself from the general verdict. Not, I hasten to add, that I consider the judgement to have been arrived at without the most conscientious consideration, or that my views, however eloquently put, would have made any practical difference.

Another controversial programme which I vividly remember was *Yesterday's Men*, a provocative but perceptive survey of prominent members of the Labour government defeated in the general election of 1970. A number of those concerned took grave exception to the programme and protested bitterly to the BBC and in the press. One of the things those years taught me was just how painfully thin-skinned politicians of all parties could be to criticism and how anxious they were for approval, not to say adulation. In fairness, most of them, unlike their counterparts in a number of ostensibly democratic countries, recognized the need for broadcasters to retain their independence. That, however, did not make them any less liable to fulminate against what they considered to be 'slanders' or 'misrepresentations', or 'unfair questioning', nor did it render them less prone to the temptation to 'domesticate' broadcasting and broadcasters in their own interests. Each party from time to time raised the possibility of tampering with the licence fee as a possible bargaining counter. I remember being taken aback by the reactions of as resourceful and battle-scarred a political operator as Harold Wilson, on whom some unjustifiable aspersions had been broadcast at about 2.30 a.m. by a disc jockey. When offered an apology, Wilson insisted that it should be broadcast at peak time. The director-general pointed out that, whereas the original remarks had been heard probably by no more than a handful of not very attentive listeners, an apology broadcast at peak time was likely to be heard by millions and would surely rebound to the prime minister's detriment. The latter was not convinced, but Hugh Greene's forecast turned out to be perfectly accurate.

The two chairmen of the BBC under whom I worked were in sharp contrast to one another in personality and outlook. The first, Lord Normanbrooke, was a former secretary to the Cabinet, with a long and distinguished record of public service. A grave, somewhat reticent man, of the utmost probity and discretion, he was extraordinarily adept at getting business through expeditiously and effectively – a chairman in a different league from most of those I encountered before or afterwards. His vice-chairman, piquantly enough, was my old chief, now Lord Fulton, who could hardly have been friendlier or better disposed towards me. It gave us both immense pleasure to have been primarily responsible for pressurizing a somewhat reluctant board of governors to allow the newly founded Open University to take over many of the BBC's employees to staff its new broadcasting services. Unfortunately, almost from the outset of his term as chairman, Normanbrooke's health was precarious and, in 1967, it deteriorated rapidly and led to his premature death.

He was succeeded by the very different Charles Hill (Lord Hill), best known for his wartime role as the 'radio doctor'. Extrovert, quick-witted, with a rich, deep distinctive voice, and a politician to his finger-tips, Hill was viewed with grave suspicion, even outright hostility, by many of the BBC staff. David Attenborough summed up the general reaction in his quip that appointing Hill as chairman of the BBC was like 'making Rommel Commander of the Eighth Army'. I always thought that was a good deal less than fair to Hill, who cherished a deep-rooted regard for the BBC and its unique place in British life. I do not think he ever forgot what the BBC had earlier done for him, and he was not as much of a stooge for Harold Wilson as was often supposed. But he was a man who succeeded in engendering a good deal of suspicion and found it difficult to win the trust of his colleagues. He was a consummate intriguer, and the way in which he got rid of Hugh Greene was typical of his methods. Relations between the two men were always extremely strained, and I believe that Hill had early made up his mind that Greene would have to go. He offered him the prospect of his becoming a governor – something that even the great John Reith had never accomplished. Hill thought this a price worth paying for getting rid of his most formidable antagonist within the corporation. Hugh Greene was within a year or two of retiring anyway and could not resist the temptation. Neither could he work with Hill, even in his new role, and after a year he retired from the board.

I had always had a profound admiration for Hugh Greene as director-general. He seemed to me to have brought a great gust of fresh air into the more than slightly stuffy corridors of the BBC. He himself aptly described the process as 'opening the windows and turning down the radiators'. He was very much a broadcasters' director-general and stood four-square for allowing them freedom and encouraging initiative. He and I always got on very well, even though, with him at 6ft 7in and me at 5ft 3in, we made an incongruous pair. He was very tickled when I once said in a public speech that we were on splendid terms although we could never be said to see eye to eye with each other! We remained good friends even after we had severed our connection with the BBC and used to meet for lunch occasionally in London.

Hugh Greene's unexpected retirement left the BBC with the tricky problem of whom to appoint as his successor. If his deputy, Oliver Whitley, had been some years younger, he would have been ideal, but there was no shortage of good candidates. There appeared to be three front runners among them: Charles Curran, director of external broadcasting; Huw Wheldon, director of television; and David Attenborough, Wheldon's second-in-command. I have no doubt at all that Attenborough was the favoured candidate of most of the people involved in making the appointment. I think it was a racing certainty that he would have got the job if he had not made it abundantly clear that he did not want 'an office job' and that his heart was set on returning to creative programme-making. Huw Wheldon had certainly made a striking success of things at Television Centre, but was perhaps regarded as being too flamboyant a personality and somewhat too loquacious. Had he been given the chance, nevertheless, I think he might have covered himself with glory. Charles Curran had been far less in the public eye than the other two, but had been an exceptionally efficient secretary to the BBC and was widely recognized as a man of strong principles, with a subtle and resourceful mind, and a superb administrator. He was unquestionably a 'safe pair of hands', even if possibly lacking in the decisiveness ideally needed in a director-general. Yet, if Attenborough remained proof against all persuasions, and he did, Curran was certainly *proxime accessit*, and it was he who was appointed. He and I were about the same age and had always been close – close enough to go to rugby matches together – and I was confident that he had what it took to make a very good director-general. Unfortunately, although he and Charles Hill were on better terms with one another than Hill and Greene had been, they were never truly compatible. Worse still, Curran died prematurely, with dreadful suddenness, before he had had enough time in the job to make the success of it of which he was certainly capable.

The board of governors was made up of a diverse group of men and women of well above average talent and experience. Two of the ablest I recall were Dame Anne Godwin and Dame Mary Green. Anne Godwin was a former trade union leader of exceptional distinction, who had been chairman of the TUC at a time when, as Charles Hill remarked, 'for a woman to get to the top she had to be abler and tougher than all the men'. She was a formidable lady, who looked for all the world like the embodiment of the old-fashioned bluestocking but could, in her lighter moments, be very amusing indeed. I was intrigued to learn from her that her great ambition, which she achieved, was to appear as a guest on Roy Plomley's programme, *Desert Island Discs*. Mary (Molly) Green was an equally able woman, but with an altogether lighter touch. She was an outstandingly successful headmistress of one of the first and largest comprehensive schools, Kidbrooke School, was a shrewd judge of character, and had an excellent eye and ear for programmes. Among the men, one to whom I was most attracted was Robert Lusty, managing director of the Hutchinson Group and a publisher with years of experience. It always seemed to me that he gave his own autobiography the wittiest of titles, *Bound to be Read*, and I read it with particular interest. He and I, too, remained in contact after we had both retired from the board and used to meet from time to time when I was in London. Learie Constantine, the West

The Broadcasting Council for Wales, June 1971. Front row: John Rowley, Mrs M. E. Jones, G.W., Miss Margaret Wooloff, Glyn Williams.

Indian cricketer, was a governor for all too short a time. A character as warm and sunny as his native climate, he was, unfortunately, bedevilled by ill health and unable to serve out more than a short part of his term. Having immensely enjoyed his recollections not only of cricket but also of many other aspects of Anglo-West Indian life and his penetrating comments on race relations, I was deeply saddened by his relatively early death. Then there was Tom Jackson, leader of the postal workers' union, a down-to-earth working-class Yorkshireman, with no frills or flounces. I found him a likeable man, but was sorry to see him subjected to such unendurable strain in the course of the 1971 postal workers' strike.

My years with the BBC greatly extended my mental horizons. I had known from personal experience as well as widely held theory that it was the corporation's function to 'inform, educate and entertain' its audience, but I had no real idea beforehand just how extensively or wholeheartedly it interpreted that brief. Nor, I am sure, had I appreciated what a worldwide influence the BBC's services commanded. Only after observing its operations at close quarters did I realize fully what an unparalleled reputation for reliability and objectivity its news services enjoyed in all countries. It was at this time, too, that I came to take in what the term 'public-service broadcasting' fully implied. Now, also, it dawned on me what a power for good the BBC had been on ITV. Certainly, I should not deny that the inception of commercial television had had a beneficial effect in some respects on the BBC; healthy competition never did any organization harm. What I think may be less often realized is how much ITV learnt from the BBC. An American friend of mine, a professor of history in the USA, who spent a year with us in Swansea as a Fulbright professor, put it very aptly when he said, 'The difference between broadcasting in Britain and in the States is that over here it is the BBC which sets the standards, so that broadcasting exists primarily to serve the public and is not all about making money.' I readily concede, however, that I do not think that that is now nearly as true as it was then.

My last year with the BBC was sadly clouded by the sudden death of my mother. She had undergone a major operation in the autumn of 1969 and came to live with us while she was recuperating. To all appearances, by the spring of 1970 she had made a good recovery and became increasingly anxious to return to her own home. Our doctor, who had been attending her solicitously, considered her well enough to do so. I took her back to Dowlais one morning in mid-April, settled her in, and stayed with her until it was time for her to retire to bed. At that point, she seemed reasonably well; but on the afternoon of the following day her neighbours telephoned me to let me know that she had died peacefully in her sleep. Her doctor afterwards told me that in his opinion she had 'come back because she wanted to die at home'. To have lost my mother as suddenly as I had my father came as a grievous shock. I felt it all the more keenly, perhaps, because I was an only child. I had loved both my parents intensely. Although they had never had much in the way of worldly wealth or position, they had both been richly endowed with those caring qualities of warmth and affection which they'd lavished on me. I was fifty years old, but I felt as bereft as any orphan child.

To intensify my despair, it was at this time that my best friend, Ieuan Gwynedd, left Swansea to go to Aberystwyth as professor of Welsh history. On the one hand, I very much wanted to see him appointed to a chair which would give him the abundant opportunities his talents so richly merited; but on the other, I was losing someone on whom I had long depended for advice and affection – more than on anyone apart from my wife. For many months I was profoundly depressed, and on the brink of a nervous breakdown. As good fortune had it, my wife and children were a great source of solace to me, and I was immensely helped also by a sympathetic psychiatrist, who seemed to have genuine insight into the sources of my neurosis. Even so, it took me about a year until I was more or less back on an even keel once more.

XI

The world of books and information

On 14 February 1973, a letter reached me from Lord Eccles on behalf of the government inviting me to become a member of the board of the newly formed British Library. Understandably, I felt elated to be asked and, provided I was given permission by the college to do so, I had little doubt that I ought to accept. For nearly thirty years beforehand, I had been heavily involved with books and libraries and had spent no small part of my time engaged in research at places like the reading rooms of the British Museum and the National Library of Wales. I confess, however, that I was not entirely sure how the college authorities were likely to react to the approach. When in 1965 the BBC had extended a rather similar invitation to me to join its board of governors, the then chairman of the college, Sir Lewis Jones, and the principal, Frank Llywelyn Jones, had been unenthusiastic to say the least. This time, however, Frank's attitude was altogether different. He put no obstacle in my way and was, indeed, warm and encouraging in his response. It may well have been that in 1965 he was new to the job of principal and had been somewhat overborne by the domineering Sir Lewis, whereas in 1973 he had been principal for many years and Sir Lewis had long been gathered to his fathers!

The board met for the first time on 16 March 1973 and turned out to be a very personable and gifted group of half a dozen or so individuals. The most worrying thing about its composition was that it had as yet no chairman, and I think that we all felt that this was not the time, nor this the vessel, to be setting off into uncharted seas without a captain. Fortunately, we had an excellent chief executive who would serve as chairman for the time being. He was Dr (later Sir) Harry Hookway, a chemist by training but a man with long experience of the world of books and information. Discreet and highly intelligent, a splendid man of business, and a cool-headed individual, he would serve the British Library uncommonly well during his years in office. He was effectively backed up during the first year or two by the board's secretary, Eddie Martindale, a civil servant long versed in the mysteries of Whitehall's ways.

We did not get our first regular chairman until December 1973, when Lord Eccles left the government to take over. He was an excellent choice. I remember Harry Hookway telling me in the course of conversation shortly afterwards that it was Eccles who had been crucial in persuading the trustees of the British Museum to agree to the concept of the British Library and that it was he more than anyone who had induced them to fall in with the proposal to allow the matchless library of the British Museum – the key piece in the whole jigsaw – to become an integral part of the new library. Harry was convinced that it was to Eccles more than to anyone else that the British Library owed its existence. Without doubt, he proved to be a good chairman of the British Library, committed to it in both mind and heart, and with a long and unrivalled knowledge of people and methods in government. I learnt a lot about the ways of politicians by listening to him and still more by watching him in action. Not for nothing had he been called 'Mr Smartyboots' in governmental circles! I well recall being in his company on the morning that the news broke of Mrs Thatcher's election as leader of the Tory Party. We had been talking about her prospects beforehand, and his view then expressed was that she was too inexperienced to defeat Heath and, of course, she was a woman. 'But,' he warned, 'it never pays to underestimate that lady.' Later, when the news of her victory came through, he smiled wryly and commented, 'I'd have done well to listen to my own advice about Mrs Thatcher.' In fairness to him, though, he was much more than a political operator. He genuinely loved books and manuscripts. He was an ardent member of the Roxburghe Club, that select company of enthusiastic collectors of magnificently bound books. When it was his turn as chairman to present a handsome volume to all the other members of that club how well I recollect his going to infinite pains to consult closely with Helen Wallis, then curator of maps at the British Museum, in order to bring out a superb special edition of an early printed atlas for the purpose.

His one big failure in relation to the British Library was his defeat at the hands of Harold Wilson's government over the site of the new building to house the former British Museum Library. It seemed to Eccles – as indeed it did to me and many others – that the site originally designated for it immediately to the south of the existing British Museum building was the ideal place. However, there were some highly influential London Labour members of Parliament who were implacably opposed to that proposal and who had convinced the prime minister that there should be large-scale development of the Somerstown site near King's Cross. In his heart, Eccles was never convinced by their arguments and some of us on the board wanted to 'go to the stake' on behalf of the Bloomsbury site, but he declined to give a lead in that direction. I think his view was that there was too much at issue and too much money involved to give the government a possible excuse for opting out altogether. Who is to say he was wrong? One thing is certain: the building cost far more than was originally planned and was subject to all kinds of delays.

During the five initial years of Eccles's stewardship, the British Library made good progress. He himself was genuinely pleased by the way it was taking shape and said so on more than one occasion. I think that what gave him special pleasure was the favourable impression it made in government circles, all the more so because a Labour administration had no cause to scratch his back! I clearly remember his last board meeting in November 1978. For a man often given to tongue-in-cheek cynicism, he spoke under the stress of deeply felt emotion. His gratitude to members of the board and the library staff appeared to be heart-felt and he was obviously much moved by the whole occasion. For my part, I had thought he might like a copy of my book on the Welsh Church as a memento, but I was taken aback that he of all people should be so touched by the gesture. Although we were very different from one another in our views on politics and society, we had got on increasingly well during the five years we had served together on the board and I was extremely sorry to see our association come to an end.

His successor, who joined the board in January 1979 was a very different cup of tea, but in his own way was just as excellent a choice as chairman. He was a very distinguished scientist, Fred Dainton, FRS, professor of chemistry at Oxford and a former vice-chancellor of Nottingham University. He had already made a profound impression on the library world by the publication of his magnificent Dainton Report, which, some years previously, had vigorously recommended the establishment of a British Library and was the 'Bible' of the new institution. I have no doubt that he was one of the best chairmen under whom I ever sat anywhere: crisp, firm, lucid, percipient and splendidly concise and businesslike in his conduct of the board – in that respect very different from David Eccles who, in his last year or two, had tended to meander self-indulgently. Seeing Fred Dainton in operation, I many times deeply regretted how mistaken the University College of Swansea had been to turn him down as a possible principal! In my first impressions of him, however, I had been quite wrong: I had thought there would be little warmth of emotion in our relationship. That turned out not to be so at all; as time went on, I learnt that beneath that apparently dour Yorkshire exterior there was a thoroughly decent and responsive heart. Although I left the board in 1980, I used to come into frequent contact with him when I was chairman of the Advisory Council and grew to like as well as respect him hugely. When he retired, it was a real pleasure for me to be asked to contribute an essay to the volume, *The World of Books*, presented to him by his former colleagues.

Members of the board were a diverse but pleasant group with whom to be associated. There were four to whom I was especially drawn: first and foremost was Alastair Ritchie, the representative for Scotland, a medical man and secretary of the Carnegie Trust there, a tall, raw-boned Scot, possessed of an endearing sense of humour; Jack Barrett, an industrial chemist, a former director of Monsanto, and another with a great sense of fun; Stephen Watson, an able historian, former Oxford don, and later vice-chancellor of St Andrew's; and John Brown, a leading member of the Oxford University Press. Considering that we had not known each other before and that many of the difficulties confronting us were not familiar to us or anyone else, we co-operated well and made surprisingly light work of our responsibilities.

The core problem facing us was to try to bring together into a single body with common aims and unified morale a group of institutions which had grown up separately and had hitherto operated as independent entities. In fairness, it should be conceded that all of them recognized the rationale for a single national library and were not unwilling to work towards achieving it. Nevertheless, each had its own autonomous tradition and its distinctive working methods and tended to view the unity now being offered them as something of a shotgun marriage. It was vital that they should, if at all possible, be persuaded to draw closer to one another in spirit as well as form. One of the better ways of helping to bring that about was to seek to preserve what was best in the existing *modus operandi* of each. Thus, for instance, it was desperately important to allay the fears of outstanding scholars employed in the library of the British Museum that it was not intended to turn them into desiccated civil servants. I think there was at first a real danger of that since, among other things, the head of the new library was, significantly, not described as a 'librarian' but as a 'chief executive' and, far from being a traditional bibliophile-scholar, was a chemist. Certainly, much of the emphasis in the new body appeared to be placed more on information and the technology associated with storing and retrieving it rather than on scholarship. Nor was it easy to instil a sense of unity and common purpose among a group of institutions not only diverse in nature but also widely scattered geographically, some of them housed in unsuitable or antiquated premises. Much of the first eighteen months or two years of the board's existence was spent in visiting the various departments so as to acquaint ourselves 'on the ground' with the circumstances in which they operated and some of the problems arising therefrom. The process proved to be an eye-opener to us all. I had never seen a library anything like the lending department at Boston Spa, which Donald Urquhart, the head of operations there, had himself designed to meet the needs of his department. It looked far more like some sort of industrial warehouse with its belt of trays endlessly moving round from section to section. But, however incongruous it might appear at first sight, it was ingeniously designed so as admirably to meet its purpose. Again, neither I nor, I believe, any other member of the board, had any idea of what conditions of low-life Victorian squalor and overcrowding lay in the dim and dirty recesses of the British Museum behind the august façades of the circular reading room or the north library. I had from time to time tut-tutted deprecatingly at the length of time it occasionally took to produce an item I had ordered at the issue desk, but having seen the desperate shortage of space and the unsuitability of accommodation in which the staff were often obliged to work, my only surprise was that they managed to produce anything at all! Another closely associated problem was that of conservation, which Nicholas Barker, head of conservation, brought out vividly for us in a most memorable presentation. All paper deteriorates and eventually crumbles to powder, but without premises that were properly ventilated and appropriately heated, there were vast quantities of printed material that would, in the none too distant future, literally disintegrate into piles of dust. This was a painful concern not merely for the British Library but for many other repositories and one to which they needed to be alerted. Given the far from ideal conditions with which many of our staff had to contend, we as members of the board were more than ever struck in the course of our peregrinations by their devotion to their profession and their determination to make a success of the new venture.

Gradually, however, the new British Library was beginning to get to grips with its tasks. At the end of the first year of its activity, both the chairman and the chief executive expressed their satisfaction at the way in which the library was settling down and more particularly at the way its various divisions were cohering as a team. By about 1976–7 there was no mistaking the impression that, however much remained to be done, the British Library was taking on meaning and purpose. In spite of a robust campaign of opposition to the removal of the British Museum's reading rooms to Somerstown, in general the opinion of the government and the users of the library was swinging round in its favour.

My first term of four years as a board member had come to an end in 1976 but was renewed for another three years. As this second term was drawing to a close in 1979, Harry Hookway urged me to consider becoming chairman of the British Library's Advisory Council, a group of some twenty to thirty figures drawn from across the United Kingdom and representative of all aspects of the library and information communities. I was glad to accept and over the next five years greatly enjoyed my contacts with a wide variety of lively and interesting people whom, otherwise, I might never have met at all. We met four times a year and discussed major issues, some of them raised by the British Library itself but many others initiated by members of the Advisory Council. At each meeting we also invited a senior member of the library staff to give us a presentation on the nature of his/her duties and the outlook for the future. Such meetings not only preserved my contacts with interesting members of the Library's staff, but also kept me abreast of what was going on in the world of books and communication. These years saw the retirement of two people who had made a contribution to the initial success of the British Library which it is difficult to overestimate – Lord Dainton and Sir Harry Hookway. The country as a whole, as well as the library, owes both of them a colossal debt.

Even in 1985, after completing my term as chairman of the Advisory Council, I still retained contact with the British Library for some years, this time as a member of a small panel which proffered advice to the library's research and development section. I found this very agreeable indeed. As it happened, the members of the panel were all old and good friends. Sir Geoffrey Elton, the celebrated Cambridge historian, I had known and respected for many years and, though he was not to everyone's liking, I always got on well with him. Then there were my very dear friends, Alastair Ritchie and Jack Spence, the latter once my close colleague at Swansea and now professor of politics at Leicester.

My years on the British Library Board and its Advisory Council, as it happened, coincided quite neatly with a spell as a member of the Advisory Council of another institution closely associated for many people with the library of the British Museum. This was the other most important repository of historical manuscripts in the capital city – the Public Record Office in Chancery Lane. The office, together with its outlying storehouses in the country, housed the unique British state archive, from Domesday Book onwards. It attracted, like bees to a hive, historians and researchers not only from all over the country but also from across the world. I had long been familiar with its rather ponderous, medieval-style architecture, and its faintly musty corridors and reading rooms, which always put me in mind of the innumerable documents and the interminable procedures of the immortal Jarndyce v Jarndyce suit in Charles Dickens's *Bleak House*. Its advisory council was made up of a small group of lawyers and historians who, it was intended, should give the staff of the office the benefit of their opinion on matters of importance referred to them, especially in relation to the dates when documents containing highly sensitive material might safely be released for inspection and study by the public.

There were a number of talented historians with whom it was a source of pleasure and enlightenment to come into contact; but, however distinguished the historical fraternity, the commanding figure, without doubt, was unquestionably the council's chairman, the Master of the Rolls, Lord Denning. Already in his late seventies and well established in the role when I joined the council, he had lost none of his formidable qualities of will or intellect. A tall, physically powerful, straight-backed man, with the countryman's ruddy, fresh complexion and the soft burr of his native Hampshire accent, he always dressed in sombre lawyer's 'uniform', with bowler, black jacket and waistcoat, striped trousers, and heavy, smartly polished black boots. It was my own impression that he envisaged running the council with as firm a hand as his own court, and while he was always polite and considerate, he brooked little or no dissent. He always began the meeting at 4.45 p.m., because his day in the courts was then over, but regardless of the fact that that was not at all convenient for those who had to travel any distance. He seemed to have no doubt that an hour or so was long enough to spend on the council and its business. We never stayed beyond 6 p.m. because that would have meant that the chairman would miss his train home and would, presumably, have been late for dinner.

There were two main topics on which we spent much of our time. The one was a hardy perennial, which cropped up over and over again in one form or another: which groups of documents ought to be kept from public scrutiny beyond the normal thirty years? Many of those suggested were quite clear-cut and there was virtually no dissent on these. There were others where the office tended to be distinctly conservative, but some of the historians would have wished to see a more flexible approach. Lord Denning almost always tended to take the side of the office, in spite of his own deserved reputation as a legal radical and reformer, perhaps because he knew better than any of us that if the staff wanted to circumvent any advice they were given it was not too difficult for them to do so. The other subject which came up far less frequently but was basically more important was the question of the new site for the Public Record Office out at Kew. The premises in Chancery Lane were, in a number of respects, cramped and antiquated, especially in relation to the seating capacity for readers and the production of documents. Even so, many historians and record researchers, including myself, were conscious of how conveniently situated the office was in central London, and, besides, regular visits there over the years had greatly endeared the old place to us, whatever its fallibilities may have been. The new buildings in Kew did not come into commission soon enough for me to have to make much use of them, although I readily admit to finding the mechanisms for calling up documents to be a vast improvement on the old system. Regular users of the place speak very well of it to me, except that they do not care much for the somewhat tedious journeys out to Kew and back!

An uncovenanted side-benefit derived from my regular visits to London which I greatly appreciated during these years was the chance of seeing both my children fairly frequently. Both were living in London for much of this time: Margaret having graduated in the University of London was later on the staff of the J. Walter Thompson Advertising Agency; and Huw, having been at university in Canterbury, was subsequently employed as an administrator at St Mary's Hospital and later at Northwick Park. In April 1977 Margaret had married a delightful young man, Scott Robertson, of whom we were all very fond and who was then on the BBC's staff in London. Although both our children were very thoughtful about ringing us up regularly each week, the opportunity of meeting them and taking them out to dinner at our favourite restaurant, Bertorelli's in Charlotte Street, was not to be missed. Many were the delectable evenings we spent revelling in each other's company even more than in Signor Bertorelli's excellent Italian cuisine.

Nearer home, I was caught up for most of the 1970s as chairman of the Pantyfedwen Trusts in succession to my old friend and mentor, Sir David Hughes Parry. Although I had been a member of the trusts for some years before his death I had never envisaged myself as succeeding him, but was heavily pressed to do so by the secretary of the trusts, Tom Jones. Tom was a successful London-Welsh businessman, who originally hailed from Blaenpennal in Cardiganshire. He had been a close friend, aide-de-camp and adviser to Sir David James, the founder of the trusts, and I found it impossible to resist his pressure. As a further inducement, he assured me, 'You don't need to worry about not having much experience of the investments of the Trusts, I'll give you all the help you need.' He was as good as his word and, during the five years of life that remained to him, we became very good friends indeed. When he died in January 1977, I was deeply distressed. At his funeral service, where I was to pay tribute to him, I was under such emotional stress that I found it difficult to speak at all. I had become extremely attached to him and felt his loss very keenly. On the way home that evening, as I drove up the hill from the Blaenpennal district to Mynydd Trichrug, there hung in the clear frosty air the most delicately thin and bright crescent moon I ever remember seeing. It was a quarter of a century ago, but I have never forgotten it and feel sure I never shall. Its elemental quality served only to intensify my overwhelming awareness of the mystery and brevity of man's life on earth. Tom's successor as the secretary of the trusts, Mansel Davies, was another splendid man, to whom I owed much, but unfortunately he, too, died very suddenly, a comparatively young man.

David James had built handsome headquarters for the trust in Market Street, Aberystwyth, and called the building 'Panty-fedwen', the name of the farm near Strata Florida where he had been born. He had lavishly endowed both trusts and called them after his mother, Catherine, and his wife, Lady Grace, and other members of his family. They were intended to work in tandem and did so quite successfully. Both dispensed charity on a larger scale than any other charity of a similar kind in Wales to a variety of good causes – religious, educational and cultural. Their members were made up of representatives of all the religious denominations in Wales and of a number of educationalists and other public figures. David James himself had, at one time, been painfully anxious to see the churches of Wales brought much more closely together and had offered them tempting financial inducements to bring that about. There were, however, too many obstacles in the path for him to achieve that goal, but the churches nevertheless benefited handsomely from the generosity of the trusts. Many places of worship received large grants to help them repair and rebuild decayed or damaged buildings, though I heard, and was not entirely unsympathetic to, arguments to the effect that helping to keep very weak churches open might not necessarily be the most effective way of helping the future of religion. One of the good causes about which there could certainly be no debate was the assistance given to the widows of ministers, most of whom had devoted a lifetime to furthering their husbands' ministries and were now in serious financial embarrassment but reluctant to plead poverty or beg for help. Nor was there any great controversy about the support being given to students in need of help to continue or complete their university or college courses. The only thing that made me, and others, distinctly unhappy in this context was that we were not empowered to give assistance to women students. D. J. James had originally intended to extend the benefits to them during his lifetime but had died before he could execute the legal documents enabling the trusts to do so. Opportunely, one of the last things I was able to do as chairman was to lead a small deputation of trustees to the Charities Commission in Liverpool to try to persuade them to broaden the terms of the trusts in such a way as to include women within them. In fairness, their response was most helpful and they granted our request. Not that the result has been entirely what was foreseen. Certainly, women have gained, but the vastly increased numbers of applicants have put much greater pressure on the resources of the trust.

A by-product of my association with Pantyfedwen which I remember with real nostalgia was the car journey from Swansea to Aberystwyth and back. For years I had the company of the Revd M. J. Williams, a non-driver who was only too pleased to avail himself of a lift; no more pleased than I was to have him as a front-seat passenger. He was the secretary of the Welsh Baptist Union and, like me, was a member of Capel Gomer. He was an ideal travelling companion: a genial personality and an admirable conversationalist, whose memory for people, events and humorous stories and episodes was legendary. He seemed to have details at instant recall of just about every chapel in Wales, most of their ministers and many of their members. One of his favourite anecdotes concerned the well-known Welsh poet and hymn-writer, Watcyn Wyn. Watcyn, it seems, was not all that talented a preacher and, when asked whether he had been invited to preach on more than one occasion at a famous chapel, replied with a beaming smile, 'No, I gave them complete satisfaction first time.' Much to M.J.'s amusement and my own, I used to like to turn that one against him on the very rare occasions when he might be one of the congregation at Capel Gomer on a Sunday morning by asking him playfully, 'Complete satisfaction somewhere this morning, M.J.?' His wife, Barbara, was also a delightful person with a highly developed sense of mischief. It would never do to ask her, 'Where's the boss preaching today?' Her invariable reply to such a query was, 'Don't ask; *I'm* the boss.'

My other frequent car companion to and from Pantyfedwen was Captain J. Hext Lewes, the Lord Lieutenant of Cardiganshire, who lived in a fine old house called Llanllŷr, once a Cistercian nunnery, just on the outskirts of the village of Talsarn. We passed his door, so it was very convenient to pick him up *en route* and set him down on the way home. He, too, had a voluminous store of stories, reminiscences and folklore, mainly relating to north Cardiganshire. Many of them were concerned with the abbey of Strata Florida and the Powel family of Nanteos. Strata Florida had, in the Middle Ages, been possessed of a renowned mazer bowl with healing powers. Following the abbey's dissolution, that bowl had passed into the hands of the Powel family of Nanteos. Captain Lewes was convinced that it had originally been the Holy Grail, brought to Glastonbury Abbey by Joseph of Arimathea himself, and had found its way thence to Strata Florida. Poltroon that I was, I never had the heart to tell him that Strata Florida had been dissolved before Glastonbury, so it was not easy to see how the transference of the fabulous vessel had come about. Not that such misgivings deterred the population of north Cardiganshire, who seem to have held the 'Nanteos Cup' in the highest esteem as having sovereign powers to heal sick people. They had been only too eager to take ready advantage of the Powel family's willingness to allow the cup to be borrowed by the populace for the purpose of restoring health to their ailing members. The problem was that over the course of time some over-eager patients had been tempted to bite bits off in order that they might have the miraculous talisman 'on call' as it were. In the end, the Powels became so concerned at the gradual deterioration of the bowl that they strengthened it with metal hoops and deposited it for safe keeping in the vaults of a bank where, as far as I know, it still languishes.

XII

Academic run-down

Although the 1970s were, in general, a difficult decade for the universities, they began very promisingly in one respect for historical studies in Swansea. That owed most to the vision and energy of a small company of postgraduate students, led particularly by Hywel Francis, and Dai Smith, a lecturer in history at Swansea, who were fired by the idea of setting up a research group to work on the history of the south Wales coalfield. Both were young, energetic, gifted men, who had long been interested in the history of the coalfield, its miners and its communities, and they were, in due course, to combine in writing a perceptive joint history of 'The Fed', the south Wales miners' trade union. They had already viewed with dismay the process by which the coalfield was being run down, with pits closing, miners' lodges disappearing, and their records and libraries being lost. A miner's son and grandson myself, I needed little persuading from them to back the project which they intended submitting to the Social Studies Research Council for a grant to enable a team of researchers to conduct intensive investigations into the coalfield and the sources of its history. The SSRC was, justifiably, convinced by their proposals and, for about three years, financed a team of four people, consisting of R. Merfyn Jones (now professor of Welsh history at Bangor), Hywel Francis (now member of Parliament for Aberavon), Alun Morgan (now an HMI) and David Egan (now head of the School of Education at University of Wales Institute, Cardiff). They worked like Trojans and compiled an illuminating report, scheduling the sources for the coalfield's history and in many instances transferring the records to safe custody in the college at Swansea. They also salvaged, where possible, the contents of the miners' libraries that were in danger of being dispersed and lost, and assembled them in Swansea. Their efforts were heavily backed by the Miners' Union in south Wales, of which Dai Francis, Hywel's father, was a most influential leader. The final outcome was the establishment, at the college, of the South Wales Miners' Library, which still exists in flourishing state. No less valuable were the numerous interviews which the team conducted with veterans from all over the coalfield. These were recorded on tape and carefully indexed. They constitute a unique source of oral history of extraordinary significance to all those interested in the history of the coalfield. Furthermore, the whole project was carried out, though unknown to its authors, just in the nick of time because, although the decline of the coal industry had been viewed with growing alarm for many years, no one could then have foreseen how frighteningly rapid the virtual extinction of this once all-powerful industry would be in the 1980s. Although much was lost, thanks to the devoted young men of the South Wales Coalfield Project a great deal was rescued for the future.

By and large, however, this was anything but a good decade for universities, and the department in Swansea ran into more than its fair share of storms. For one thing, we lost a number of colleagues and friends whose departure we could ill afford. Among those who had left us were some who were crucial to the development of recent Welsh history, on which I had set such store. Kenneth Morgan had gone to a fellowship at Queen's College, Oxford; Ieuan Gwynedd Jones went to become pro-fessor of Welsh history at Aberystwyth, and was followed there a year or two later by John Davies; while Dai Smith moved to Cardiff. All four continued to produce work of first-class quality and Welsh history gained enormously thereby, but the team which had been assembled in Swansea and which had collabor-ated so fruitfully and in such harmony, was seriously weakened. Fortunately, among those still left were Drs Ralph Griffiths, Prys Morgan, Peter Stead, David J. V. Jones, David W. Howell and Ifor

Rowlands, all of whom were dedicated scholars. Gareth Elwyn Jones, a former student and then a lecturer in education, was another who contributed handsomely to Welsh history. Happily, also, there were other members of the department, like Dr Muriel Chamberlain, David Walker and Neville Masterman, none of whom could be described as Welsh historians, but all of whom made notable side-contributions to the history of Wales. One of the setbacks which caused me most distress was the steady decline in the health of my professorial colleague, Alun Davies. He had been diagnosed as suffering from diabetes and the neuropathy associated with it worsened in the 1970s. He remained remarkably brave and cheerful and was as delightful a companion as before, but he could not do much more than maintain his teaching, which was of an exceptionally high quality. He was not able, however, and could not be expected, to put the kind of effort into directing international history with that early dynamism and commitment he had shown in the 1960s and which he – and I too – had once hoped he would continue.

Money grew increasingly tight in the college, and soon after Professor Robert Steel had succeeded Professor F. Llewelyn Jones as principal of the college, one of his earliest decisions was to set up an economies committee to cut down drastically on expend-iture wherever possible. He asked me to act as its chairman, but I thought that really should have been his job and told him as much. He, not unreasonably perhaps, felt he was too new to Swansea to take it on and preferred to entrust the responsibility to someone who knew the college better, so I agreed to do it. It was a task that did not make me many friends; everyone com-mended economies in principle as long as they themselves were not affected – the NIMBY (not in my backyard) maxim was very conspicuously in evidence! Within a year or two, I also found myself acting as one of Steel's three vice-principals. The other two, Ivor Isaac and Jim Burke, both scientists, were splendid men and old friends. I was especially well disposed to Ivor, a Swansea man, an old student of the college, whose family were on affectionate terms with my own. Principal Steel tended to depend heavily on his vice-principals and liked to have regular and frequent meetings with them. I used to call the group 'the kitchen cabinet', a piece of nomenclature which went down well with the rest of them. The registrar, Aneurin Davies, a former Aberystwyth student, was also someone I had known for many years and got on with famously, which was a distinct help to a vice-principal. The principal was an unusually kind and considerate man, with whom I enjoyed teaming up, but the experience convinced me that I did not care all that much for administration. I had no doubt whatsoever in declining Robert's pressing invitation to continue for at least another year as vice-principal. I had come more and more to appreciate why John Parry had, many years before, given up administration and returned to history.

Money was in increasingly short supply in the University of Wales as well as in the college. The Board of Celtic Studies, of which I had been chairman for some years, experienced the economic pressures and had to look for ways of reducing any unnecessary expenditure. It appeared to me essential that we should make up our minds what were our most important core activities and ensure that they were carried on uninterruptedly while reducing expenditure on less essential outgoings. Clearly, the most vital task was the work on the university's Welsh dictionary, and we succeeded in keeping the editorial team intact. Professor Caerwyn Williams, the honorary consultant editor, and Gareth Thomas, the university registrar, and one of his successors Alan Kemp, were my staunchest allies, to whom I owed a great debt. The work of bringing out the instalments in which the dictionary was published was arduous and slow, but it is encouraging to see that the dictionary is now almost complete. The other enterprise of a similar kind which I wanted very much to see preserved was the national atlas. In this instance, one could hardly have improved on the man in charge – Professor Harold Carter – who brought the whole project to a successful and relatively speedy conclusion. I also judged it necessary to ensure that the board's research periodicals, the *Bulletin of the Board of Celtic Studies*, *Llên Cymru*, *Studia Celtica* and the *Welsh History Review*, should continue to appear. What had to be dispensed with, unhappily, was the appointment of research assistants, which had been initiated some years earlier. The scheme had been of real assistance to a number of established scholars and had also had the effect of recruiting a number of promising young people. It proved possible, however, for the committees of the board to maintain the production of occasional monographs. I was delighted to see the history and law committee launch that series known as 'Studies in Welsh History', edited by Kenneth Morgan, Ralph Griffiths and myself. It still flourishes and has been responsible for twenty volumes so far, on average about one every two years. They cover a broad and miscellaneous range of topics within the whole span of the history of Wales and have met with an encouraging response. They provide not only an additional resource for the study of Welsh history but have given a body of young historians encouragement in their studies and the hope of seeing their researches appear in print. What gave me great satisfaction was that the first two volumes were written by two of my most gifted former students, Dr F. G. Cowley and Professor Geraint H. Jenkins, the third by Dr John Davies and the fourth by Professor Merfyn Jones, formerly of the South Wales Coalfield Project. It has often occurred to me that it was a pity that such a series did not exist in earlier times so as to give wider circulation to the contents of many a promising thesis – flowers born to blush largely unseen and wasting their sweetness on the desert air.

This was about the time when the board adopted the initiative proposed jointly by the Oxford University Press and the University of Wales Press to publish a series of volumes on the history of Wales, which it was hoped might achieve for Wales something like what the Oxford History of England had done for England. The members of the history and law committee were not of one mind about the feasibility of this proposal. Some of the most senior and distinguished among them were of the opinion that the time was not ripe to venture on a standard account of the whole history of Wales. But a majority of us were in favour of pressing on with the scheme and we entered into discussions with the OUP. The latter were anxious at first that it should be encompassed within four volumes, but, after a great deal of discussion and debate, finally agreed to six. The confidence of those members of the history and law committee who wanted to proceed with the series has at least been partially justified, in so far as four out of the six volumes have been published and the remaining two are well on the way.

It was not only the academic world which experienced the onset of change and economic shortfall; local government was also undergoing extensive reorganization. The changes brought about in 1974 confronted the *Glamorgan County History* with formidable challenges. Happily, my confrère, Dr (now Professor) Ralph Griffiths had been appointed secretary in 1971 and he proved to be a tower of strength in the years that followed. We had succeeded in publishing Volume III, *Medieval Glamorgan*, edited by T. B. Pugh, in 1971, and, in the same year, a reprint of Volume I, *Natural History* (originally published in 1936). But the changes of 1974, when the old county of Glamorgan was split into three parts, East, Mid and West Glamorgan, raised awkward questions about whether or not the new county councils would consider themselves committed to the financial undertakings entered into by their predecessors. One of the first things that had to be done was to make a presentation to them of extracts from the reviews which had been written of Volumes I and III. As it happened, those reviews had been universally favourable – even glowing – and certainly helped to convince the county councils that the venture was worth backing.

I was deeply relieved to hear the news, since I had been hard at work on Volume IV, *Early Modern Glamorgan*, for many years and the volume was ready to go to the press. I had had to write nearly half of it myself because some of those who had promised contributions had withdrawn. I was, by this time, acutely aware of how appropriate to the fate of an editor of a county history was the phrase, 'the loneliness of the long-distance runner'. Nevertheless, it was my good fortune to have unusually helpful printers in the persons of the two Sansom brothers, Robert and Arthur, of Qualitex Printing, Cardiff. Experts in their craft, they and their employees took exceptional pride and interest in printing the *History of Glamorgan* and could not have done more than they did on the technical side. As far as the mechanics of editing the text, compiling the index and correcting the proofs were concerned, my wife had been unbelievably helpful with Volumes III and IV, and would go on being so until the whole venture was completed. Volume IV was published late in 1974 and was generously received by the reviewers. Two commentators, in particular, gave me a deep sense of gratification. Joel Hurstfield, Astor professor of history in University College London, for whose intellect and character I had immense respect, reviewing the volume in a long and thoughtful piece in the *English Historical Review*, described the book as 'a delight to the mind, stimulating, wide-ranging and illuminating'. J. H. Parry, our former principal, also sent me a most encouraging letter from Harvard, in which he said the book was all that he had expected it to be – and more!

Volume II was at this time proceeding very slowly, but I did not feel at all worried about it. It was in the safe hands of Dr H. N. Savory, an archaeologist of long experience and great distinction. He had emphasized from the beginning that he thought it would be very unwise to publish a volume on the archaeology of Glamorgan until such time as the Ancient Monuments Commission had published its proposed inventories of the county's archaeological remains. That was reasonable enough, but it did mean a very long delay, which was compounded by the death of some contributors and the withdrawal of others. I had implicit confidence in Hubert's editorial talents, however, and felt sure that he would ultimately bring forth a splendid volume. My faith in him was rewarded and was buttressed also by the financial assistance made available to us by the National Museum, thanks to the good offices of Dr Douglas Bassett, the director, and Dr David Dykes, the secretary. The volume was published and launched at a ceremony held in the museum in 1982, and proved to be a handsome and valuable study.

Volumes V and VI raised intractable problems, though. Volume V, *The Economic History of Glamorgan*, was in the care of Professor A. H. John, a Glamorgan man and professor of economic history at the LSE. I thought from the optimistic reports I was getting from him, at admittedly infrequent intervals, that the work was progressing favourably. What I did not know, and neither did anyone else, it seems, was that his health was declining badly, but he was understandably reluctant to admit that to other people. By 1978 I had had to press him much harder to give me a completion date, since it was essential to keep the county councils reasonably happy with the progress of the venture. In October 1979 he arrived in Cardiff with only three of the twelve chapters. Three weeks later, I heard the tragic news that Arthur had died very suddenly. I went up to LSE to go through his papers with a mutual friend, his colleague, Theo Barker, but we could find no trace of the missing chapters; nor did they ever turn up. I could hardly ask anyone else to take on the editing job, so there was nothing for it but to assume the responsibility myself. I shall always feel exceptionally grateful to Colin Baber, of University College, Cardiff, who gave me quite extraordinary help over the next two years, which enabled me and the team of contributors to get the volume out by late 1981. It was a great relief to all of us to see that, in spite of all the upsets encountered while it was being produced, reviewers and the general public were exceedingly generous in their reactions to it.

Volume VI, *The Social History of Modern Glamorgan*, was being edited by one of the most brilliant of Welsh historians, Professor Gwyn Alfred Williams. We had been born and brought up in the same town and had known each other well since we were children. I had been overjoyed when Gwyn had agreed to take on the volume and was convinced that he would carry it out superbly. As ill luck would have it, however, he told me that he was sorry, but I would have to look for someone else as editor. This was a profound disappointment to me; especially when I discovered that we should have to start from scratch again with the volume. Fortunately, my colleague, Dr Prys Morgan, was willing to be persuaded to undertake the work instead of Gwyn. I have had reason to feel profoundly indebted to him for doing so, even though the volume could not be completed until 1988. He assembled an enthusiastic band of mainly young historians and brought out an excellent volume, which was widely ac-claimed. With this, the six volumes of the *Glamorgan County History* were finally completed; the first of the county histories of Wales to be brought out after the Second World War. I had 'served' a 'sentence' of thirty years' hard labour – about twice as long as I had initially bargained for, but it was a task well worth undertaking in my opinion.

The 1970s had also seen me being invited to deliver a number of interesting lectures, the most prestigious of which were a talk to the annual meeting of the Historical Association at Bangor, the O'Donnell Lecture in the University of Edinburgh and the four colleges of the University of Wales, and a talk to the annual meeting of the Association for the Advancement of Science. The latter was not, I need hardly add, a scientific discourse but a lecture to the anthropology section on the cult of St David. It was the BBC Annual Radio Lecture of 1976 that was the most significant, however. I was intrigued when the Controller Wales, Owen Edwards, asked me if I would be willing to take as my subject 'The Welsh in America' to commemorate the second centenary of the American Declaration of Independence. At a much earlier stage in my career, when I was engaged on a short biography of Samuel Roberts, Llanbryn-mair, the subject had fascinated me, and I had often thought I should like to return to it. Here was an admirable opportunity to do so and, though I had deserted the field for twenty years or more, I gladly re-entered it and gave a radio talk on *A Prospect of Paradise? Wales and the United States, 1776–1914*. When the BBC and the Honourable Society of Cymmrodorion took the unusual step of combining to publish the lecture in Welsh and in English, I was delighted. It also made me realize that for many of the lectures I had delivered in the 1970s, I had been concerning myself with the relations between religion, language and nationality in Wales, to such a degree that I thought that together those lectures which had been published and a number of others still in typescript might make a worthwhile book. I put the idea to John Rhys, then director of the University of Wales Press, and he enthusiastically accepted the suggestion. The outcome was the publication of a book which was never planned but just happened, *Religion, Language and Nationality in Wales* (1979). Of many kind comments on it, the one I most valued was that made by my fellow professor of history at Cardiff, Stanley B. Chrimes, a splendid friend but not one usually given to extravagant turns of phrase.

He wrote me a letter, which I still cherish, describing it as 'a collection of absolutely *first-rate* [his italics] essays . . . so lucid, so perceptive, expressed in admirable English'.

Even so, I felt that there was something bitterly ironic in the fact that the year in which I had ventured to publish studies of Welsh national consciousness down the ages should also have been the same one in which the Welsh people voted heavily against devolution in the referendum of 1979. Like many Welsh historians – foremost among them, Gwyn Alfred Williams, I imagine – I had looked forward with keen anticipation to a vote in favour. What I had never expected was a four to one majority against, although I recollect that a conversation I had had with Lord Heycock a few months before the vote took place had made me much more cautious. I should have expected him to be in favour of devolution but found, in fact, that he was quite unsympathetic. What shook me even more was his estimate of a vote of at least three to one against. I felt uncomfortably sure that his views were in line with a large body of Welsh Labour opinion. Even a later conversation with Ted Rowlands, MP, who was much more favourable to devolution, did little to reassure me. When the voting figures were announced I found myself pondering why everything had gone so badly wrong – from my point of view, anyway! Obviously, there were many people in Wales who could not be expected to be in favour of devolution and had never concealed their distaste for the idea. What I found much more puzzling, though, was why so many who, one might have supposed, would be inherently in favour had voted against. Clearly, there was a large body of Labour opinion firmly opposed to the idea in spite of its being put forward by their own party; Llew Heycock had been a typical example. Even in north Wales, where strongly Welsh sympathies might have been expected to be in evidence, there were many against. That, I could only conclude, had arisen from a suspicion that, in any new representative body, south Wales would have a dominant voice, one less sympathetic to the interests of the north, possibly, than a London regime. I also suspected that perhaps the most powerful conviction, though one not all that frequently or openly expressed, was the idea common to all parts of the country and people of all shades of political opinion, and none, based on experience of the local government changes of 1974, that devolution would mean another layer of government, involving more demands for money with little or nothing in the way of benefits to show in return. Whatever the reasons for the result, I could not help being deeply dismayed by the thought that, as Welsh people, we had turned our backs on a glorious opportunity. At the time, I should never have thought that, less than twenty years later, we would get a second chance.

I myself had had two chances of changing course in the 1970s, neither of which came to fruition. The first had cropped up in 1975 and presented a possibility of moving to St David's College, Lampeter, as its principal. When the post was first advertised, I was not at all interested. Then I came under pressure from two quarters: first, from Steven Watson, principal of St Andrew's and my colleague on the British Library Board, and later from J. R. Richards, bishop of St David's and president of Lampeter. The latter was so keen that I thought he was virtually offering me the position, so I began to think seriously about it. Ever since John Parry had gone to Harvard, I had always been aware that there could be acute tension between the rival demands of history and administration. I was still sorely divided in my own mind, but I had persuaded myself that at St David's, Lampeter, a very small college, it might be possible for me to carry on with my writing as well as being principal. I think that the underlying sense of unease and uncertainty must have been evident when I was being interviewed. I had a very unconvincing and lacklustre interview, and I am sure that had I been a member of the interviewing committee I would not have voted for the indecisive character I presented that evening. When Dr B. R. Rees was declared the successful candidate, I felt a sense of relief rather than disappointment.

The second opportunity emerged in 1978, when Aberystwyth was looking for a successor to Sir Goronwy Daniel. This time I really was invited to become principal by the president of the college, Lord Cledwyn. It was something I had to think about in all seriousness. Lord Cledwyn was someone whom I had long known and for whom I had enormous respect and liking; and the same was true of his vice-president, Sir Melvyn Rosser, who was also associated with the invitation. Aberystwyth was the oldest of the colleges of the University of Wales; I myself had been educated there and I owed it great debts of gratitude. It was also put to me that it was my 'patriotic duty' to accept. Some of my dearest friends, people like Ieuan Gwynedd Jones, J. E. Caerwyn Williams and Graham Lloyd Rees, were on the staff there and they were urging me to accept. Yet I knew from the beginning that if I was going to be honest with the college and myself, I should have to turn it down. Three years as vice-principal in Swansea had confirmed my opinion that I was not really cut out for academic administration. Additionally, I was having worrying troubles with my health – notably from prolonged insomnia, and from a serious rise in blood pressure, from which my father had suffered and which had hastened his death at the relatively early age of sixty-one. But the decisive factor was Fay's view that it would be a mistake for me to accept. She knew me and understood me better than anyone else, and she was sure in her own mind that I should become increasingly worried and ill at ease with myself if I gave up scholarly activity for full-time administrative duties. I thought that I ought not to go against her opinions and I have never regretted that decision. Having later come into close contact with Dr Gareth Owen, who was appointed principal in 1978, I am sure that the college chose wisely and well.

Another Aberystwyth election in which I had been involved was that of the professor of history in 1977. The man then chosen had appeared to me, and to others who knew him well, to be tailor-made for the post. That was Robert Rees Davies, a highly gifted historian who had begun his career in my department in Swansea. A Welsh-speaking Welshman, trained in London and Oxford, who after Swansea had spent most of his time at University College, London, he was young, vigorous and full of bright ideas. Sadly enough, there were a number of people at Aberystwyth who regarded his appointment as a 'Swansea fix' because three of us on the appointing committee had Swansea connections – Ieuan Gwynedd Jones, Kenneth Morgan and myself. It was certainly true that we had all three regarded Rees as being easily the strongest candidate, though not because we had been his colleagues at Swansea but on grounds of his sheer ability. I felt I could sympathize with him more than most because he was going through the same sort of misfortune that I had encountered twenty years earlier in Swansea. When reviewing his book, *Lordship and Society in the March of Wales*, in the *Western Mail* a short time later, I went out of my way to emphasize to the critics and the doubters that Aberystwyth 'could take the warmest pride in its young professor of History; his tenure of that chair is likely to be a profoundly memorable one'. It was, indeed, and it has since led him to a fellowship of the British Academy, presidency of the Royal Historical Society and the Chichele professorship at All Souls College, Oxford.

One of Rees's closest friends in Swansea, and subsequently in London and Aberystwyth, was Professor Alun Davies. Alun was not only the most companionable of men, but also an exceptional teacher and, potentially, a great historian. Ill health was, however, to dog his footsteps throughout the 1970s, and especially from 1975 onwards, and it prevented him from achieving anything like his full potential. Increasing debility meant that, even with the most strenuous efforts, it was as much as he could do to keep his schedule of lectures and tutorials going. The bright hopes we had both entertained when he first came to Swansea of his being able to give greater thrust and more sustained impetus to new departures in international history were now seen to be incapable of fulfilment. Having been close friends with him for forty years or more, I felt more than ordinarily downcast by the decline of his health. By 1978 it had become evident to him and his devoted wife, Margaret, that their efforts to keep him on course academically could no longer be sustained. His doctors were emphatic in their advice that he should retire at the end of the session in 1979. All the rest of us in the department and, indeed, in the college, were deeply distressed at the prospect of losing him, and were still more saddened by his death in March 1980. He had faced the last harrowing illness of cancer with quite exemplary calmness and courage, typical of a man who had battled bravely with cruel ill health over many years.

Alun's death was only one of a number of losses to befall me at about this time. Ivor Isaac had died in 1978 soon after retiring as vice-principal; Arthur John went within months of him; early in 1980 I was shattered to hear of Charles Curran's sudden death; and Alun died in March. John Rees, one of the most genuine and principled people I ever knew, went late in 1980, and John Ithel Jones died about the same time far away in Australia. All of them were youngish men, about my own age or a little older; all of them were men whose friendship had been unutterably dear to me. Coming in quick succession, the loss of each was a painful reminder of my own mortality. All the more so, because I was uneasily aware that my father had died when he was sixty-one, and I had an apprehensive intuition that I might very well go at the same age. So it was hardly surprising that when, in 1981, the college put forward an attractive scheme for early retirement for those of its members over sixty years of age I should have been eager to participate in it. I had always intended to retire in 1984–5, when I should have completed forty years' service in the college, and, in view of the prospects of the cutting back and economies likely to be operated, it no longer seemed to me to be worthwhile hanging on.

These last years were not all doom and gloom, though. In my final year as head of the department, it gave me great satisfaction to press for Ralph Griffiths to be made a professor. His promotion was merited not only on the grounds of his outstanding contribution to scholarship but also of his dedicated efforts in all aspects of the work of the department: lecturing, tutoring, planning and administration. I was also much exercised by the consideration that there should be someone of professorial rank in the department who would have a genuine concern for the well-being of Welsh history after I had gone, and I knew that in the current climate of economies that could only be achieved by internal promotion.

In 1980 it was very enjoyable to be elected president of the Cambrian Archaeological Association and thus to follow in a very distinguished line of succession. For my presidential address, I took Bishop Henry de Gower as my subject, partly because he was a man from the Swansea district and one of the most renowned bishops of St David's, but chiefly because he

175

was, in my opinion, Wales's greatest medieval builder, if not, indeed, her finest builder of all time. In the New Year Honours List of 1981 I was awarded a CBE. I have never known just why I should have been given it then, nor who was responsible for submitting my name, but I am truly grateful to them for thinking of me all the same.

An even more exciting event took place in January 1981 when our first grandchild was born. Our daughter, Margaret, gave birth to a little boy. To my intense pleasure, his parents decided to call him Daniel James, the names of my father and my mother's father. He was not called after them, but the fact that he shares their names has always given me great joy. He has a charming sister, Elinor, who is two years younger than he. Our son, Huw, also got married in the early 1980s to one of his colleagues at Northwick Park. His wife, Hazel, is a lively and attractive lady, who has established herself very securely in our affections. She and Huw also have two delightful children, both girls, called Nia and Eleri. All four of my grandchildren are immensely dear to me and have been a source of unending happiness and interest.

My cup really overflowed in 1984, when I was presented with a book of essays in my honour, edited by four colleagues who had worked with me in Swansea – Ieuan Gwynedd Jones, Rees Davies, Ralph Griffiths and Kenneth Morgan. They had assembled a formidable team of contributors, who combined to put together a magnificent body of fourteen essays and a bibliography, entitled *Welsh Society and Nationhood* and published by the University of Wales Press. They contrived to keep the whole project a secret from me until the very last moment and then presented the volume to me at a delightful informal gathering of friends, associates and colleagues in the senior common room at the college in Swansea. It was a gesture which I have always valued beyond words and which touched me more deeply than I can readily express.

XIII

Clearing up the backlog

When I retired early, my fixed intention was to devote myself very largely to writing. Like many other retired people, I had naïvely supposed that my time would now be very largely my own, thus enabling me to forge ahead with those projects which I had especially wanted to complete but for which I had never hitherto been able to find sufficient leisure to carry through. Weighing heavily on my mind was the need to finish off two substantial volumes, long promised but not completed: the badly delayed book on Wales during the years from the end of the Glyndŵr Rebellion in 1415 to the outbreak of the Civil Wars in 1642, the third volume in the Oxford series on the history of Wales; and the even more belated study of Wales and the Reformation. However, like many others who take retirement and look forward to a blissful spell of largely uninterrupted leisure, I found it did not work out quite like that. Not that I am going to indulge in that facile cliché, 'I wonder how I ever previously found time to go to work.' I do not have much patience with people who say things of that sort; I cannot believe that they ever worked really hard at their jobs! But I did discover that I was still committed to quite a heavy stint of lecturing: to schools and educational establishments; to broadcasting organizations; to societies, large and small; and to religious bodies and places of worship. In spite of shaking off college and departmental responsibilities, I also found not only that I was still involved in a variety of former administrative commitments but that it proved to be impossible to refuse some new ones.

G.W. with Professor Gareth Elwyn Jones at the Welsh History Resources Committee, 1990.

It would be wrong of me not to confess that I relished much of the lecturing and teaching I used to do. One of the things that I discovered almost at once was how badly I missed my contact with students. It was not at all difficult to keep up my links with former colleagues, but it was virtually impossible, without sticking my nose into departmental activities, which I scrupulously sought to avoid, to maintain my association with students, except for a few research pupils, whom I still had left. As with so many things in life, it was only when I was deprived of these pleasures that I fully appreciated just how much they had meant to me. That was especially true of my contacts with students. I cannot claim to have been an outstanding lecturer or an exceptional tutor, but I did get a tremendous kick out of the company of students over the years. I found that their energy, enthusiasm and liveliness kept me younger, better-humoured and more buoyant than I should otherwise have been. Even now, I still treasure the companionship of many of those former students with whom I have been able to keep in touch.

What has also been extremely rewarding has been to continue affording such help as I could to many other historians and authors. I have especially enjoyed reading and commenting on the work of former students, like Professor Gareth Elwyn Jones. In spite of an appalling accident he suffered in 1992, which has since confined him to a wheelchair, he has gone on studying, writing and editing in the most gallant manner. I call to see him pretty regularly and am always filled with admiration by the uncomplaining courage and cheerfulness that he and his wife, Kathleen, invariably display. They are two of the bravest people I have ever known. Two of my other former pupils to whom I am especially attached are Dr W. S. K. Thomas, who has produced an excellent series of books on aspects of the history of Brecon and Breconshire, and Dr Fred Cowley, who has written extensively on church history. A more unusual association is that with Professor David Farmer, an authority on business management. I could never have given him the slightest help with his books on management, but we have found a great deal more in common with his books on Swansea and its district. He is another who battles heroically against illness and has become one of my most treasured friends. Another is Dr T. G. Davies, an eminent psychiatrist who has an insatiable interest in the history of his native west Glamorgan. He has written a number of fascinating books on the subject, and it has been a privilege and a pleasure for me to contribute a foreword to them. An association that I have esteemed as much as any has been that with Professor F. Smith Fussner and his wife, Jane. The Fussner family spent a year with us in 1964–5 when Smith was a Fulbright professor. Since they have been back in Oregon, USA, we have maintained a regular correspondence with them. Both Smith and Jane were the most thoughtful and engaging of correspondents, and their letters have not only been a pleasure but an education. Jane, alas, died some years ago in tragic circumstances, but I still write to Smith and his daughter, Lisa. There are many others with whom I keep up contacts which I value greatly.

In addition to my college teaching and associations, I had always revelled in talking to adult education groups, branches of the Historical Association and all kinds of historical societies, big and small. I had assumed that I should carry on with, and even increase, this sort of activity when I retired. There were some groups to whom I lectured at frequent intervals, including some of the county history societies, like the Glamorgan History Society or the Carmarthenshire Antiquaries Society; in fact, there is not a county history society in Wales to which I have not lectured at least once. Many other groups were smaller and more localized, like Swansea's Royal Institution of South Wales, the Neath Antiquarians, the Dulais Valley Historical Society, or the Merthyr Tydfil Historical Society. What appealed to me very much was the opportunity of talking to sixth-form groups or educational seminars, because this enabled me to absorb again something of the aura of undergraduate teaching I missed so badly. There was a sixth-form conference held annually at the Mid Glamorgan Residential Centre at Ogmore, which I found more than ordinarily attractive, and when these premises were in danger of closure some years ago I reflected on the huge benefit the centre had conferred on pupils in the whole locality.

There were other more celebrated bodies whose invitations to lecture to them conferred a considerable privilege on the recipient. One such was the National Museum of Wales, which asked me to deliver its 75th Anniversary Lecture in 1982. That was all the more prestigious because the lecturer at the twenty-fifth anniversary had been Sir John Edward Lloyd and, for the fiftieth anniversary (at which I had been present), Professor R. T. Jenkins. To follow in the footsteps of two such illustrious pioneers of the history of Wales was an inspiring but, at the same time, a slightly daunting prospect. Similarly, it was a thrill for me to celebrate the fiftieth anniversary of the British Council in Wales in 1984 by lecturing on 'Wales and the world', however intimidating the field encompassed by the title! Three memorial talks I was pleased to undertake were the Griffith John Williams Lecture at Cardiff, the R. T. Jenkins Lecture at Bangor and the Stephen J. Williams Lecture at the Neath National Eisteddfod. It was an honour to give them, not only because I had had such admiration for the range and depth of the scholarship of all three, but also because I had been so fond of them as individuals.

What gave me the deepest satisfaction, though, was the British Academy's invitation to give the John Rhŷs Memorial Lecture in

1983. Although such great historians as Sir John Lloyd and Sir Goronwy Edwards had given earlier lectures in the series, it was language and literature scholars in the main who had been asked. Mine, too, for that matter, was on a theme which spanned the realms of literature and history, being concerned with the relationship between religion and Welsh literature in the age of the Reformation. What pleased me most was the kind note sent to me within a few days of my delivering the lecture by the president of the Academy, Professor Sir Owen Chadwick, who had been my chairman for the occasion. In it he wrote, 'after a considerable experience of listening to lectures, I can say that that was one of the best I ever heard . . . there was not an instant in which my attention was not gripped.' That lecture may greatly have helped when, two years later, I was elected a fellow of the Academy. Fellows are enjoined to maintain strict confidentiality concerning nominations for fellowship and the details of elections. They certainly did so in my case, and I did not know then, or now, who had been responsible for putting my name forward. I had no intimate contacts with influential personalities in the so-called 'golden triangle' of Oxford, Cambridge and London, which counted for so much in the choice of fellows in those days. In more recent years, the Academy has made con- scious efforts to broaden the scope of election. Even so, I am not unaware that there have been a number of scholars at least as talented as I who have not been singled out for election to the fellowship.

The years 1985, 1987 and 1988 turned out to be very busy ones. In 1985 there were widespread celebrations in Wales to mark Henry Tudor's victory at Bosworth in 1485, which generated a whole crop of requests to talk about Henry, his Welsh connec- tions, the battle and his accession to the throne. Two years later, it was the turn of the quadrennial international conference of Celtic Studies to meet in Wales, and we were only too happy to organize the week's meetings in Swansea on the theme of 'The Celts and the Renaissance'. Over 300 delegates from all parts of the world, including such unexpected places as the USSR and the Far East, attended what proved to be a very successful and enjoyable week of meetings. To be asked to give the opening plenary lecture was a delight for me, as indeed was the exercise of editing the proceedings of the conference, *The Celts and the Renaissance: Tradition and Innovation* (Cardiff, University of Wales Press, 1990), which Robert Owen Jones, the hardworking secretary of the conference, and I undertook jointly. The year 1988 saw a double celebration: the 400th anniversary of both the defeat of the Spanish Armada and the publication of the first Welsh Bible. Looking back on the many discourses on both subjects to which I gave vent in English and Welsh, the most memorable trio seems to have been those given at Plymouth, Cambridge and Tre'rddôl, Cardiganshire. The first was one on Philip II and the Armada to a special Historical Association conference at Plymouth; the second was at St John's College, Cambridge, of which William Morgan was an alumnus, on 'William Morgan and the Cambridge connection'; and the third was at Tre'rddôl Museum, Cardiganshire, where the National Folk Museum arranged a talk by me in Welsh on 'The European background of the Welsh Bible'.

Three years later, the Honourable Society of Cymmrodorion conferred on me the honour of awarding me its medal, which is possibly the highest cultural distinction that Wales can bestow on one of its own sons. I received it on 19 October 1991 at the National Library of Wales, along with the scholar and littérateur, Professor Gwyn Jones, and the artist, Kyffin Williams. To be admitted in such company to that élite band of Welshmen who had previously been chosen for this distinction was, indeed, a privilege. For forty years I had had a close and invigorating association with the society, having published my first papers in its *Transactions*, lectured to it on a number of occasions and been a member of its council. I was presented by Dr Peter Roberts of the University of Kent, who performed the duty with characteristic grace and felicity. I was more than grateful for the generous things he said about me, but I especially appreciated the tribute he paid to Fay for her crucial share in what I had achieved.

There are three comparable distinctions which have also meant a great deal to me. Two of them were honorary fellowships of the colleges with which I have been most closely associated: Swansea and Aberystwyth. The third was the honorary degree of Ll D of the University of Wales. What made it all the more gratifying was to have been presented by long-standing and very dear friends, Ralph Griffiths (Swansea and the LlD) and Kenneth Morgan (Aberystwyth). It is always very agreeable, if slightly embarrassing, to hear complimentary things said about one, but they mean more when they come from men who have known you for a long time, have worked closely with you and had ample opportunity of getting to know you.

Along with those lecturing commitments that I assumed in retirement, I had expected to have to continue for some years with the gaggle of administrative responsibilities I had acquired outside the college. What I had not bargained for was that I should pick up a number of new ones. One of the latter was to become president of the Association of History Teachers of Wales. Since this body was founded to inspire and to help teachers of history in the schools and colleges of Wales, it was one calculated to spark a lively enthusiasm in me. It motivated me all the more because it sprang from the keenness of a group of my former pupils, whose ambition it was to infuse new life and purpose into history teaching in Wales. I found their zest and determination irresistible and, for many years, served as president of the association and as chairman of the Welsh Joint Education Committee's subcommittee for the encouragement of the publishing of sources for teaching Welsh history.

Round about this time, too, I succumbed – not at all un-willingly – to the solicitations of Dr David Dykes, then secretary of the National Museum of Wales and soon to be its director, that I should assume the chairmanship of the committee of the National Folk Museum at St Fagan's (now the Museum of Welsh Life). I have always regarded St Fagan's as one of Wales's most distinctive and distinguished institutions. I derived a lot of pleasure from co-operating with the two curators there in my time, Dr Trefor Owen and Dr J. Geraint Jenkins. The activities of St Fagan's and its staff were congenial to me, and I should have been glad to continue in the post of chairman for some years longer than I did. Sadly, however, I fell out irreconcilably with some of the officers of the National Museum itself over what I considered to be the unfair treatment they had meted out to Dr Dykes and felt that I had no option but to resign.

An altogether more unexpected move came from the direction of some leading civil servants in the Welsh Office, with whom I had had close associations as a member of the Historic Buildings Council. They pressed me strongly in 1983 to take the chair of the Ancient Monuments Board in succession to Professor Sir Idris Foster. During the first year or two of my period as chairman, I had a distinctly rough ride. I discovered that some of my colleagues on the Board regarded me with more than a little suspicion and distaste as a stalking horse, possibly even a 'stooge', for the civil servants. As time went by, however, the realization dawned on them that I was not a 'secret agent' nor had I a private Welsh Office 'agenda'. Tension slackened markedly, new members joined the board, and the ten or twelve years I spent as chairman proved very agreeable.

Being chairman of the Ancient Monuments Board carried with it membership of the small executive committee of the new body, Cadw, set up by the secretary of state for Wales to oversee all his responsibilities for the built heritage of Wales. Cadw's first chief executive was John Carr, a man in whose appointment I had had a small share and who became one of my closest friends. We met each other frequently, not only on the Cadw committee but also in the meetings of the Historic Buildings Council, the Ancient Monuments Board, the Royal Commission for Ancient Monuments and the new education subcommittee which John set up to extend Cadw's influence among schoolchildren by arranging courses and events for them. He lived in Pennard, just outside Swansea, and was generous in giving me lifts to and from meetings. Travelling together as frequently as we did, just the two of us in John's car, we got to know one another unusually well and enjoyed each other's company immensely. I have always been deeply impressed by John's calm wisdom, his profound common sense and his endearing flashes of good humour. I consider that he did a superb job as chief executive of Cadw; and if I had to say which I believe to be his two greatest achievements I should not hesitate to choose his acquisition and restoration of the finest Tudor house in Wales, Plas Mawr at Conwy, and the admirable series of guide books to the monuments of Wales for which he and Dr David Robinson were responsible.

Bidding farewell to Cadw, 1994. G.W. with the chairman,
Sir Wyn Roberts.

Cadw's chairman was another whom I got to know very well: this was the minister of state for Wales, Sir Wyn Roberts (later Lord). Although we were far apart in our views on politics, that never prevented us from being the best of companions. Wyn was an excellent chairman: relaxed, good-humoured and very effective at getting through the business. He was also whole-heartedly committed to the work of Cadw, something that could not be said of most politicians.

In 1986, the Royal Commission on Ancient and Historical Monuments (Wales) was faced with an unforeseen crisis when our chairman, Professor Richard Atkinson, suddenly informed us that he felt obliged to resign as the result of medical advice. This was a bitter blow; Richard, as well as being one of the country's leading archaeologists and author of a classic work on

The Chairmen and Secretaries of the Royal Commissions on Ancient Monuments, England, Wales and Scotland, 1989.

Stonehenge, was an experienced and first-rate chairman. As the longest-serving of his colleagues, I tried all I knew to persuade him to stay on, even if it meant appointing a deputy to take his place for a few months. All in vain! He was adamant that he must give up all his public activities and husband his failing physical resources. All the members of the commission were desperately sorry to hear the news and, as his colleague on the commission for a quarter of a century, I believe I was more upset than anyone. Reluctantly, I agreed to take his place, but on the strict understanding that it would be for four years only, until I reached the age of seventy.

In that same year of 1986, nearly fifty years after I had first entered the college at Aberystwyth as an undergraduate, I was overjoyed to renew my connection with it as one of its two vice-presidents. I was already very familiar with the president, Sir Melvyn Rosser, and the principal, Dr Gareth Owen, and during the years that followed we collaborated harmoniously and fruitfully. When Dr Owen retired in 1988, he was succeeded by Professor (now Lord) Kenneth Morgan – an appointment which gave me unbounded delight. Having known Ken so well for the thirty years since he first came to Swansea as a young research lecturer, and having watched with increasing pleasure and admiration the way he had matured into one of the most accomplished British historians, I thought Aberystwyth had made an inspired choice. The ensuing years of his principalship served only to underline that conviction. The sudden and tragic death in 1992 of his young and charming wife, Jane, at the age of only forty-two might well have shattered many a lesser man but, to his eternal credit, Ken, distressed though he was, refused to let his private grief get the better of him. He continued to fulfil his duties as principal as conscientiously and with as much application as before, and rendered the college four more years of service as well as writing a full-scale biography of James Callaghan. I have seldom been as profoundly moved by such courage and devotion. Jane had been a research pupil of Ieuan Gwynedd, who wrote a moving tribute to her in a book of essays entitled *Social Policy, Crime and Punishment: Essays in Memory of Jane Morgan* (University of Wales Press, 1994), published in her memory and jointly edited by Ieuan and myself.

The principal of Aberystwyth since 1995 is one alongside whom I served for only one short year, but that was more than enough to convince me that, by temperament, interest, erudition and outlook, he is ideally fitted to give impetus to the college. Furthermore, Dr Derec Llwyd Morgan has as his president Lord Elystan Morgan, an ideal successor to one of the ablest and most honourable of college presidents, Sir Melvyn Rosser. I came to appreciate the sterling qualities of Elystan's mind and character when we operated together in double harness for five years as vice-presidents of the college, under Melvyn's presidency.

Nevertheless, the principal focus of my attention during these years of retirement had been writing history, to which I have devoted most of my time and energy. I have always enjoyed writing and I am never as happy as when I can sit at my desk and concentrate uninterruptedly for hours at a stretch; reminiscent of the duke of Gloucester's jibe at Edward Gibbon's expense, 'Another damned, thick, square book! Always scribble, scribble, scribble!' Oddly enough, though, the first book I produced after retiring was not one I had foreseen but one which arose from a chance remark made to me by the avuncular Huw Lewis of Gwasg Gomer (Gomer Press, Llandysul), who said to me in teasing tones, 'You've never entrusted us with publishing one of your books.' His shaft went home; for the next week or two, I ruminated long and hard about what he had said and turned over in my mind the possibility of bringing together a number of historical essays I had written in Welsh; some of them already published in various journals, others still in manuscript. I sent them to Gwasg Gomer for their consideration and was heartened when they agreed to publish them in a volume of some two hundred and forty pages called *Grym Tafodau Tân* (The Power of Tongues of Fire) (1984). My continuing misgivings about writing in Welsh were, to some extent, allayed when the book was subsequently awarded an Arts Council prize.

Its success also emboldened me to take up another unexpected invitation, this time from the University of Wales Press, to write a short bilingual book on Henry Tudor and Wales, destined for the series they used to produce for schools in celebration of St David's Day – like the one I had written thirty years earlier on Samuel Roberts. What pleased me most about the preparation of this book was the opportunity it gave me to retrace Henry's landing in Milford Haven, the route of his march through Wales and England, and the site of the battlefield at Bosworth. The book having been duly published on St David's Day, 1985, I was encouraged to learn that some three thousand copies of it had been sold within a relatively short space of time.

It was now high time, however, to turn to weightier projects and, in particular, to the Oxford University Press series on the history of Wales, which was urgently calling for attention. It had got away to a flying start in 1981 with the publication of, paradoxically, the last volume chronologically, on Wales from 1880 to 1980, which its author, Kenneth O. Morgan, had called *The Rebirth of a Nation*. It had been universally well received, and no general editor could have asked for a better initial volume. I knew that by 1985 two other authors were well on course to complete their assignments. Rees Davies let me have the manuscript of his volume on Wales from 1063 to 1415 before the end of the year. I was so struck by its range and clarity that I could not help concluding that, if John Edward Lloyd had set the tone in the twentieth century for the history of medieval Wales, then Robert Rees Davies had no less certainly done so for the twenty-first. It came as no surprise to me when the book was awarded the prestigious Woolfson Prize a few months afterwards. Geraint H. Jenkins had sent me the manuscript of his volume on Wales from 1642 to 1780, *The Foundations of Modern Wales*. This, again, was a joy to read, bearing as it did all the hallmarks of wide-ranging scholarship and a lucid and engaging style. Like Rees's work, it was characterized by the fresh outlook of a rising generation of Welsh historians, and it seemed to me to be a worthy companion to the volumes already published in the series. I could not but feel sincerely grateful to the authors of these volumes for the generous tributes each had paid me for my help as general editor of the series; but, at the same time, I was acutely conscious of what a privilege it had been for me to be associated with three such brilliant colleagues. My one regret was that, priced at £40, a demanding sum at that time for a book of Welsh interest, these volumes were unlikely to sell as well or to obtain the readership they deserved. But all my efforts to persuade OUP either to reduce the selling price or, better still, to bring out a paperback edition, went for nothing at the time. Not until they had disposed of most of the original hardbacks, some six or seven years later, would the Press consider bringing out paperback versions.

Along with the volumes by Rees and Geraint, my own contribution on the history of Wales from 1415 to 1642 had also appeared in 1986. I admit that I had hoped it would have seen the light of day some years before this, and the publication of Ken's volume in 1981 had been a standing reproach to me. All I can say in mitigation is that the years from 1978 to 1982 had been traumatic ones for me, and that I had found it virtually impossible to settle to the task of sustained writing until 1983. I had also found the chapters on the fifteenth century – possibly the most neglected period in the medieval history of Wales, or the history of England for that matter – unusually difficult to organize, let alone to write. Still, by 1987 four out of the six projected volumes were in print and all had been enthusiastically welcomed. I should greatly have liked to see the two remaining ones appear within a short space, but they, it must be admitted, seem to have been dogged by misfortune from the outset: prospective authors have been struck down by illness or mischance and have had to drop out and be replaced by others who have, in turn, not found it easy to fulfil their commitments. However, at the time of writing both are now well under way and should not be much longer delayed. Even while we await their appearance, I think it no more than just to express gratitude to the Oxford University Press, the University of Wales Press and the Board of Celtic Studies for having persevered so long with the enterprise. The doubting Thomases who initially argued that the time was not opportune for so ambitious a venture have been proved to have been, if not wrong, unduly pessimistic. It has been shown to be possible to bring out a range of standard volumes on the history of Wales which will bear comparison with those undertaken for other countries. It seems to me that they have proved very valuable – especially in paperback format – to teachers in colleges and schools, to individual researchers and to interested lay readers. They are an integral part of the 'renaissance' in the history of Wales.

At this point I had hoped to pick up my work on Wales and the Reformation once more. The Leverhulme Trust lent a sympathetic ear to my request for funds and awarded me an emeritus fellowship so that I might spend some time at various major repositories. Alas, as Robbie Burns so rightly observed, 'the best-laid schemes o' mice an' men/Gang aft a-gley'. I was unexpectedly sidetracked by an improbable combination of the Swansea Corporation (especially its leader, Councillor Tyssul Lewis), some of my colleagues at the college and the enterprising local publisher, Christopher Davies. They were all bent on seeing a book published on the history of modern Swansea since the Industrial Revolution. I sympathized with their aspirations to such an extent that I allowed myself to be talked into editing the projected volume, and I have never regretted that decision. The corporation was honourable in its financial support; Christopher Davies proved to be a dedicated publisher, who spared no effort to bring out a handsome volume, lavishly illustrated and at the extraordinarily tempting price of only £15; and the contributors who wrote the various chapters played their part nobly – and punctually! *Swansea: An Illustrated History* (Christopher Davies, 1990) is a book with which I am deeply proud to have been associated; I regard it as a small requital of the huge debt I owe the city which has been home to me and mine for more than half a century.

In the early 1990s, also, there were two other books, with which my ever-loyal allies, the University of Wales Press, became involved. The first was a collection of essays on a variety of topics concerning religion in Wales, which appeared under the title of *The Welsh and their Religion* (1991) and bearing the imprint of the press. The most significant contribution was a seventy-two-page survey of the history of religion in Wales, 'Fire on Cambria's Altar'. This had begun life as a single lecture but had been expanded into three, which were delivered at Cardiff and Bangor. A number of people had urged me to publish them, but publication presented me with an awkward problem: they were too long for a journal article and too short for a book. I extricated myself from the dilemma by offering the press 'Fire on Cambria's Altar', along with five other essays all on various aspects of religion in Wales and including the John Rhŷs Academy Lecture. Together, they made up a handsome volume. The second book was a short biography of Owain Glyndŵr, which I had written many years before at the request of Charles Mowat for the Clarendon Biographies series he edited for the Oxford University Press. It was not conceived of as a profound work of scholarship but was intended primarily for school pupils aged about fifteen to sixteen. The University of Wales Press, however, considered that it could be brought up to date and extended somewhat. I also changed the title from *Owen Glendower* (given it by OUP) to *Owain Glyndŵr*, and it was under that guise that it emerged in 1993. I have been pleasantly surprised by how well it has sold; no doubt, celebration of the sixth centenary of the rebellion in 2000 helped no end.

At long last, I could devote my undivided attention to Wales and the Reformation. For years I had come to envisage myself as some kind of unholy combination of the Ancient Mariner and the Flying Dutchman – the Ancient Mariner because it had increasingly seemed to me that I should never get this albatross of a book off my neck, and the Flying Dutchman because I had set sail on so many occasions without once reaching my destination. I used to say to Fay that I thought she must more than once have felt as desperate as the poor heroine, Senta, in Wagner's opera, with that spectral 'vessel' having floated around for so long without assuming tangible form as a published book. Happily, she had never once been reduced to the pitch of throwing herself over the cliff in despair, but I suspected that she must, on many occasions, have been sorely tempted to push me over! Finally, after close on fifty years of intermittent toil and trouble, the manuscript was complete. I admit to being a very poor judge of my own work; when it is finished, I never seem able to tell whether it is any good, and I am always tempted to believe it is sub-standard. Over the years, I have learned that I am not alone in this respect. I have been reassured to discover that at least three people whose work I intensely admire have had similar misgivings. I remember no less a prose artist than Kate Roberts once telling me that she always had grave doubts about the quality of her own writing, and I know that Rees Davies and Ieuan Gwynedd Jones go through what Ieuan calls 'black nights of the soul' about their efforts. I have even come across very distinguished historians who could not bring themselves to release their typescripts to the printer because of their invincible misgivings! Long and laboriously as I had toiled over *Wales and the Reformation*, I felt I could have done with several more years on it, but was driven to the conclusion that, however much time I spent on the 'fine tuning', I should never be wholly satisfied. So I decided that, whatever its shortcomings might be, it was better that the book should be published than that perhaps it should never see the light of day at all as the result of still more procrastination. One thing is certain: whatever blemishes there are in the text – and there may be very many! – its format and appearance could hardly have been improved upon. The University of Wales Press, even by its own high standards, excelled itself in the quality of its production. I have cause to be

Investiture at Buckingham Palace, 1996.

eternally grateful to the Press; of all the many books it has published for me, this one, I thought, was quite the most striking in its visual impact. I could not have wished for a more handsome offering to round off a lifetime of research and writing. I have also been deeply touched and reassured by the reaction of many readers that they have found it to be a book for which it was worth waiting so long.

By a remarkable coincidence, as I completed the text of *Wales and the Reformation* in 1995 and had just sent it to the publishers, I was awarded a knighthood. I do not suppose for one moment that anyone in the ranks of the Establishment knew about the book, so whatever the reasons for the honour may have been it could not have been a 'long service medal' for work on the Reformation. The justification given for it in the official announcement was that it had been awarded 'for services to the history, culture and heritage of Wales', which was a more nicely turned compliment than I could ever have supposed that anyone would pay me. It came at a uniquely appropriate moment in my life and I am duly grateful to those anonymous figures behind the scenes who had sufficient belief in me and my efforts to put my name forward.

XIV

Retrospect

Looking back over a life which covered some eighty out of the hundred years of the tumultuous and swiftly changing twentieth century, I must, on balance, regard myself as having been fortunate to live *when* I did and *where* I did. The fact that I was born in the twentieth century and that I lived all my life in the 'developed' world has to be accounted a great boon. As a historian, I am more than ordinarily aware, I suppose, that I was born into a world which saw a vastly improved material standard of living when set side by side with the conditions prevailing in earlier centuries. As compared with all periods down to about the end of the nineteenth century, the quality of life expectancy, health, diet, clothing, housing, heating, sanitation, domestic appliances, conditions and hours of work, leisure and mobility of people in the twentieth century had advanced beyond measure. For centuries, our forebears had been obliged fervently to pray unceasingly, 'from war, plague and famine, good Lord deliver us' – those dreaded horsemen of the Apocalypse always so frequently and terrifyingly in evidence! Although far from having been totally subdued, the depredations of two of those perennial enemies had at least been much reduced.

Nor am I, as a historian, less conscious of the blessings of having lived in a free society. I know only too well that the majority of the human race has always lived – and still lives – in societies where the freedom of the individual is extremely limited, if not non-existent. I suspect that many of us forget, or possibly have never been aware of, what an extremely rare exception in the human story is the existence of a free society. Whatever the limitations or weaknesses of our western democracy may be, it brings with it the inestimable prerogative of free expression, free association, free worship and all those other freedoms we perhaps take too readily for granted, although, heaven knows, we have witnessed all too often the suppression that some governments can impose upon their unhappy subjects in the contemporary world. Freedom from such tyranny to be able to pursue one's intellectual interests and to publish the conclusions without being subjected to control or censorship should be of cardinal priority to those who work in universities, and to none more than historians.

One of the most notable features of twentieth-century Britain has been the unmistakable improvement in the educational opportunities open to the children of ordinary people. I was born to working-class parents in 1920, and my generation was only the second to proceed in any considerable numbers through the whole gamut of state education in elementary and secondary schools and university. Certainly, those of us who did so were still no more than a small minority, who owed much not only to our own intelligence and effort but probably even more to the willingness of parents to sacrifice on our behalf and to encourage us to persevere. That was undeniably true of me. I do not maintain for a moment that my parents were not anxious to see me obtain a better job and a higher standard of living than they had had. What was out of place in that, anyway? But I can honestly say that what counted for still more in their eyes was that I should be afforded the chance of making the most of any educational opportunities of which I was capable of taking advantage. I have always been, and still remain, inexpressibly grateful to them for their attitudes, values and encouragement, about which they never made any song or dance.

I know – let it be said without demur – that in earlier ages, I might have been put in the care of a farmer or a craftsman and could well have absorbed from him the standards and ability of a man who worked with his hands as well as his mind. Who is to say that I might not have been a better and more rounded individual for such an apprenticeship? As it was, I was vouchsafed the opportunity to enter into a learned profession, and for that I have always been abidingly indebted. The duties it called on me to perform were profoundly satisfying and I found myself being paid to carry out some responsibilities I should have been only too pleased to undertake voluntarily. I still count it providential that I should have been appointed to a university post at a time when entrance to that profession was so rare and chancy. It gave me the opportunity to embed myself in a life's work which proved to be immensely rewarding – not financially, perhaps, but emotionally and intellectually, without doubt. Reading, teaching and writing have given me indescribable pleasure down the years, and my associations with pupils and colleagues, inside my own department and outside it, have been a joy unparalleled. Administration has, assuredly, been something of a 'curate's egg', good in parts but far from wholly satisfying. One of the unmixed blessings of a university life has been the possibility of continuing with some of its fulfilling activities long after retirement: research and writing *a fortiori*, even though there has been no choice but reluctantly to recognize the awareness of a perceptible slowing down and a gradual waning of the powers, intellectual and creative.

What made my career as a university teacher all the more congenial was that I spent it all in Swansea. I have always found the college and the city most agreeable. Like so many of Swansea's inhabitants we have always lived on the hill, with a panoramic view of the sea and all its changing moods and colours, which have been an unfailing source of attraction and refreshment to me in daylight and at night. Placed as we are at the gateway to Gower, that entrancing peninsula long officially recognized as an 'area of outstanding natural beauty', and within easy reach of the moorland and mountain solitudes of the West Glamorgan upland country and the Brecon Beacons and the Black Mountains, we have been blessed indeed. Swansea's climate, it has to be conceded, is damper, or 'softer' as our Irish friends would say, than might ideally be wished, though it has the merit of being mild and genial, with significantly few of winter's rigours in the shape of snow or frost.

The city and its environs are home to a warm-hearted, friendly, welcoming people, with a strongly Welsh-speaking element in their midst, which I have always found to be one of the most endearing attractions of the area. Throughout all my years here I have maintained my membership of a Welsh-language chapel and have reaped rich harvests, social as well as spiritual, from doing so. The one thing that distresses me deeply, though, has been the steep decline in the membership not only of my own place of worship but of all the Welsh-speaking chapels of the district, some to such a pitch as to have shut their doors for good.

The withering of religious belief and worship has been, of course, only one of the tragic aspects of twentieth-century existence. Worst of all is that it should have been subjected to the holocaust of two world wars, and innumerable lesser ones, including many long and lamentably savage and destructive civil conflicts. Because of the exponentially increased human capacity for decimation and the total mobilization of whole societies to wage war, the carnage and havoc caused among civilians as well as armies have been nightmarish and have made the twentieth century the worst ever for the destruction of human life. For fifty years, mankind has lived under the apocalyptic shadow of the atomic bomb and the Cold War. In the course of more than one crisis – Berlin, Korea, Suez, Hungary, Cuba, Indo-China and others – like countless millions of others across the globe, I shuddered at the prospect of annihilation, possibly even the extinction of the whole human race.

War has been by far the greatest, but not the only, threat. My childhood, along with that of numberless others, was spent amidst appalling economic blight which, by a cruel irony, only the approach of the Second World War did anything much to alleviate. Hundreds of millions of the planet's poorest populations, dwelling in the underdeveloped countries of the world, are still enveloped by such conditions. Overpopulation, disease, malnutrition, lack of sanitation and educational opportunities, exploitation and misery remain as seemingly immovable features of their daily scene. Efforts to bring about a more equal access to, and sharing of, the world's resources make painfully slow, or no, progress, as do all attempts to achieve sustainable economic growth and some measure of control over the earth's finite resources in place of the Gadarene rush to satisfy consumerism's insatiable demands.

Yet, however dire these overhanging perils may be, the instinct of most of us, no matter how absurdly unjustified it may appear in the light of cold, rational calculation to be, is to resist the temptation to despair, if only because there is so little any of us can do seriously to alleviate the dangers, whether as individuals or in organized groups. Instead, we turn, as men and women have always done, to such sources of comfort, human or divine, as are known to us, and with their help to create tiny oases of delight in the world's wilderness. For my own part, religion, nature, history, literature, music, art and attempts at writing have been the most creative and therapeutic influences in my life. I continue to believe in the existence of a benevolent deity. The friendship and loyalty of others, by example far more than precept, have also contributed enormously. Above all, the unwavering love of my wife, children and grandchildren has given me more true happiness than I could ever hope to put into words. In spite of the long catalogue of horrors seen, heard of and experienced in my lifetime, and for all the soul-chilling uncertainties to which any contemplation of the future must give rise, I believe I can nevertheless say with the Psalmist, 'the lines have fallen to me in pleasant places'.

Index

Aberfan disaster 140
Aberystwyth 10, 41, 42–6, 48–50,
    52, 55, 56, 58, 59, 60, 62, 72,
    88, 106, 147, 159, 160
  Alexandra Hall 45–6
  Fairlea, Loveden Road 45, 46
  University College of Wales 10,
    41, 42ff., 48, 73, 74, 76–7, 82,
    89, 91, 94–6, 112–13, 163,
    172–4, 183, 186–7
Adams, Samuel 33, 38
Amis, Kingsley 97
Ancient Monuments Board 184
Anglesey, Henry, marquess of
    121–2
Anglican Church 10–11
Association of History Teachers of
    Wales 183
Association of University
    Teachers 86
Atkinson, Richard 186
Attenborough, David 141, 143,
    144, 145

Baber, Colin 169
Bangor 91, 106–7, 120, 123
Baptists (*Bedyddwyr*) 10, 11
Barker, Nicholas 154
Bassett, Douglas 168
BBC 60, 82, 132, 136–8, 139, 141,
    142–4, 146–7, 149, 170
  Cardiff studios 60, 82, 134, 139
  London 134–5, 140, 141
  Wales 138, 140–1, 170
Bethania Chapel, Dowlais 11
Bevan, Cecil W. L. ('Bill') 52
Bibliography of the History of Wales
    120
Bowen, Roderick, MP 1–3
Brecon, Breconshire 3–5
Brecon Beacons 109, 197

British Academy 174, 181
British Library 105, 149, 150–1,
    154–5, 156, 172
  Advisory Council 152, 155, 156
British Library, British Museum
    88, 105, 149, 150–2, 153–5, 172
Broadcasting Council for Wales
    60, 132, 133, 134, 136–7, 140
Buchedd A, *Buchedd* B 12–13

Cadw 184, 185
Caeharris 4, 9, 11
Cambrian Archaeological
    Association 175–6
Capel Gomer (chapel), Swansea
    99, 160, 198
Cardiff 22, 29, 52, 60, 90, 91, 92,
    106, 109, 138, 163, 169, 171
Cardiganshire 42, 43, 52, 124, 158,
    161
Carmarthen, Carmarthenshire 43,
    99, 118, 140, 180
Carmen 23
Carr, E. H. 54, 56
Carr, John 184
Carter, Harold 165
Celtic Studies, Board of 90–1, 92,
    112, 119, 120, 165, 166, 190
  international conference on
    Celtic Studies (1987) 181–2
Chadwick, Sir Owen 181
Chamberlain, Muriel E. 112–13,
    164
Charles, Prince of Wales 139–40
Chrimes, Stanley B. 111, 170–1
cinemas, Dowlais 13–14
Cledwyn, Lord 172
coal industry 4, 13
conscientious objection 56
Constantine, Learie, Lord 145
Cowley, Frederick G. 96, 166, 179

Crawshay family 26, 31
Curran, Sir Charles 144, 145, 175
Cyfarthfa Castle Grammar School
    26, 27, 28, 29, 30, 31, 33, 34,
    38, 40, 63, 67
Cyfarthfa Park 31–2, 64
cymanfa ganu 11–12
Cymdeithas yr Iaith Gymraeg
    (Welsh Language Society)
    124, 138–9
Cymmrodorion, Honourable
    Society of 170, 182

Dainton, Frederick, Lord 152, 155
Daniel, Sir Goronwy 172
Davenport, Ada C. 39–40
Davies, Alun 106, 111, 113, 116,
    164, 174–5
Davies, Alun Oldfield 60, 132,
    133–4, 135, 140
Davies, Aneirin Talfan 135, 140
Davies, Aneurin 165
Davies, Christopher 190–1
Davies, David E. ('Jim') 124
Davies, David John 33, 37–8,
    40–1
Davies, Elwyn 16
Davies, Evan Lewis 33–4
Davies, Gwladys 25–6
Davies, Hywel 132–3, 134–5
Davies, James Conway 105
Davies, John 114, 163, 166
Davies, John Edwin 33, 35
Davies, Margaret 106, 174
Davies, Richard (1501–81) 59, 62,
    91–2
Davies, Robert Rees 114, 173–4,
    176, 188–9, 192
Davies, Thomas G. 179
Davies, Vivian 27
Denning, Lord 156–7
devolution referendum (1979)
    171–2
Dickens, Charles 156
Dic Penderyn 14, 22
Dillwyn (Swansea) Building
    Society 128

Dodd, Arthur H. 91, 106–7
Dowlais 1–6, 9–10, 11–16, 17, 23,
    30, 43, 45, 128, 147
  choir 68
  library 37
  market 4
  people 3
  Works 18
Dykes, David 168, 183

Eccles, David, Lord 149–52
economic depression 3, 7, 11, 13,
    15, 198
Edward, Prince of Wales (Edward
    VIII) 7–8
Edwards, Charles A. 75, 78, 84–5
Edwards, John Ll. 52
Edwards, Sir J. Goronwy 82, 91, 181
Edwards, Owen 170
Egan, David 162
Elton, Sir Geoffrey 155–6
English, English-speaking 3, 10,
    20, 50, 90, 112
Erddig and the Yorke family 122–3
Evans, Elizabeth (grandmother)
    22–3, 24, 25, 29
Evans, Evan D. 52
Evans, Gwynfor, MP 139–40
Evans, Harry 23
Evans, James (grandfather) 14–15,
    22–3, 24, 25, 29, 176
Evans, Ronald G. 27–8
Eynon, John 122

Farmer, David H. 179
Farrington, Benjamin 96–7
Festival of Music and the Arts,
    Swansea 126, 128–9, 130–1
Foulkes, Colwyn 122
Francis, Hywel, MP 162
Fulton, John Scott, Lord 85–6,
    93–4, 104, 110, 117, 143
Fussner, Frank Smith 179

general election
  (1945) 80
  (1970) 142

General Strike (1926) 14, 22
George, T. Neville 19
Gibbon, Edward 126, 187
Gilwern 5–6
Glamorgan 3, 102, 119, 197
Glamorgan County Council 118, 167
Glamorgan County History 118–19, 167–9, 170
Glamorgan (Local) History Society 100–2, 118, 180
Godwin, Dame Anne 145
Godwin, H. James 80–2
Gower 79, 100, 197
Gower Street, London 105
Gowerton 73, 79
Gray, Thomas 21
Green, Dame Mary 145
Greene, Sir Hugh 133, 134, 142–3, 144, 145
Greenway, William 96, 114
Griffiths, James, MP 126
Griffiths, Ralph A. 120, 163, 166, 167, 175, 176, 183
Gross, Joseph 4, 65
Grym Tafodau Tân 188
Guest family 4
Guest, Keen and Nettlefold 20
Gwernllwyn Chapel, Dowlais 12, 26

Hardie, Keir, MP 15
Heath, Archie 96–7
Heller, Erich 97
Heolgerrig 9, 66
Heycock, Llewellyn, Lord 171
Higher certificate 40
Hill, Charles, Lord 143, 144, 145
Hill, Herbert 79
Historical Association 70, 180, 182
Historic Buildings Council 120–1, 123, 184
honorary fellowships 182–3
Hookway, Sir Harry 150, 155
Howell, David W. 162
Hughes, Cledwyn, Lord 126, 173
Hughes, Ernest 92, 107

Humphreys, Emyr 50
Hurstfield, Joel 106, 111, 168

inaugural lecture 111–12
Independents (*Annibynwyr*) 10, 11
Institute of Historical Research 105, 106
Investiture (1969) 139
Irish people ('Plant Mari') 9–10, 14
iron industry, ironworks 6, 13
Isaac, Ivor 164, 175
ITV (independent television) 136, 147

James, Sir David 158, 159–60
James, Myra Bowen 65, 70–1
Jenkin, Thomas J. 49
Jenkins, David 12–13
Jenkins, Geraint H. 166, 189
Jenkins, Robert T. 91, 92, 107, 111, 180
Jenkins, Mr and Mrs Tom 46–7, 56
John, Arthur H. 119, 168–9, 175
John, Richard, 118–19
Jones, David J. ('Gwenallt') 9, 51
Jones, David J. V. 163
Jones, Emrys Wynn 165
Jones, Evan J. 97
Jones, Francis 106
Jones, Frank Ll. 119, 164
Jones, Gareth Elwyn 164, 178, 179
Jones, Gwent 100
Jones, Gwilym P. 88
Jones, Ian P. ('Dan') 47
Jones, Ieuan Gwynedd 93–4, 96, 104, 112, 147–8, 163, 173, 174, 176, 187, 192
Jones, John R., 97, 110
Jones, Kathleen 179
Jones, Sir Lewis 75, 117, 149
Jones, R. Merfyn 162, 166
Jones, T. Gwynn 46, 51
Jones, Thomas (professor) 54
Jones, Thomas (Pantyfedwen) 158–9
Jones, Vernon 80

justice of the peace 126–7

Kenvin, Arthur 27–8, 29, 60–1
Knowles, David 87, 116

Labour Party 14, 15, 126, 142, 151,
    171
Lampeter, St David's College 44,
    172
lectures, lecture notes 75, 111
Leverhulme Trust 104, 190
Lewes, J. Hext 161
Lewis, Alun 50
Lewis, Clement 44, 45
Lewis, Edward A. 54, 55, 59, 71, 95
Lewis, Frank R. 50
Lewis, Henry 74, 78, 89, 95
Lewis, Huw 188
Lewis, Rex 47
Lewis, Saunders 124
Lewsyn yr Heliwr 14
Llandaff 134, 136
Lloyd George, David, Earl 8
Lloyd George, Owen, Earl 122
Lloyd, John D. K. 122
Lloyd, Sir John E. 106, 116, 118,
    180, 181, 189
Lloyd-Johnes, Herbert J. 121
local government 167–8
London 88, 91, 104, 105, 106, 107,
    108, 109, 113, 132, 134, 135,
    141, 157–8, 171
London School of Economics
    (LSE) 106, 113, 169
Lusty, Robert 145

manuscripts 87–8
Margaret, Princess 134
Mary, Aunt 9, 13
Masterman, Neville C. 93, 164
Merthyr Express 14
Merthyr Intermediate ('County')
    School 30, 62, 63–6, 68–9, 70,
    73, 78
  teaching staff 66–7
Merthyr Public Library 37, 71
Merthyr Riots (1831) 3, 14, 22

Merthyr Settlement 38
Merthyr Tydfil 3, 9, 15, 19, 23, 26,
    27, 30, 63, 67, 180
  Choral Society 68
  Historical Society 180
Methodists (*Methodistiaid
    Calfinaidd*) 10
military service 56–8, 60
Minchinton, Walter E. 93, 94
Morgan, Alun 162
Morgan, Derec Ll. 187
Morgan, Elystan, Lord 187
Morgan, Jane 187
Morgan, Kenneth O., Lord 112,
    120, 163, 166, 174, 176, 183,
    186–7, 188–9
Morgan, Prys T. J. 163, 169–70
Morgan, Thomas J. ('T.J.') 116
Morgan, Victor 79, 110
Morrell, William P. 63, 65–6
Morris, Hettie 38–9
Mowat, Charles 108–10, 191
Mumbles Head 77
music 23–4, 128–9

Namier, Sir Lewis 126–7
Nanteos 161
National Eisteddfod of Wales 12,
    51, 137, 180
National Library of Wales 53, 54,
    72, 88, 91, 104, 149, 182
National Museum of Wales 91,
    168, 180, 183–4
National Trust 122, 123
Neale, Sir John 91, 99, 106
Neath Opera Company 43, 130,
    180
Nonconformity 12
Normanbrooke, Lord 143

Owen, Gareth 173, 186
Owain Glyndŵr 191
Oxford University 82, 105, 153
Oxford University Press 116, 153,
    166, 177, 188–90
  History of Wales series 166, 177,
    188–90

Pant 16, 18, 20
Pant School 5, 16–18, 20–1, 25–6, 29, 30, 71
Pantyfedwen Trusts 158–60
Pantysgallog 18–19
Parry, Sir David Hughes 124–6, 158
Parry, John H. 110, 117, 165, 168, 172
Parry-Williams, Sir Thomas H. 51, 53–4, 55
Peate, Iorwerth C. 89
Penguin books 37
Penywern 10, 39
Philipps, Sir Grismond ('Jack') 121
Pierce, T. Jones 91, 111, 116
Plaid Cymru 139
poetry 38, 129
Pontsarn 5, 18
Pontsticill 5, 19
postgraduate research 59, 62, 66, 71, 82, 87–8
Public Record Office 88, 105–6, 156–7
Pugh, T. Brynmor 119, 167

Quinn, Alison 78, 83
Quinn, David B. 74, 75, 78, 83, 89, 94–5, 104, 107–8, 110

radio broadcasting 135–6
railways 17, 18, 19
Rees, Graham Ll. 96, 173
Rees, Sir James Frederick 100–2
Rees, John C. 110–11, 175
Rees, William 91, 95, 118–19
Reformation, Protestant 87
in Wales 62, 71, 89, 94–5
Religion, Language and Nationality in Wales 170
research supervisor 73, 88–9
Rhys, John 170
Rhŷs, Sir John, Memorial Lecture 181
Richard, Henry, MP 15
Richards, John R., bishop of St David's 172

Richards, Thomas 91
Ridd, Thomas, 96
Ritchie, Alastair 152–3, 156
Roberts, Glyn 83, 91, 107, 111, 120
Roberts, Kate 192
Roberts, Peter 182
Roberts, Robert O. 93–4
Roberts, Samuel, Llanbryn-mair 89–90, 170, 188
Roberts, Sir Wyn (later Lord) 185
Robertson, Daniel James (grandson) 176, 199
Robertson, Elinor (granddaughter) 176, 199
Robertson, Scott (son-in-law) 158
see also Williams, Margaret N.
Rosser, Sir Melvyn 173, 186
Rowlands, Edward, MP 171
Rowlands, Ifor 163–4
Rowley, John 135
Royal Commission on Ancient Monuments 120, 123, 168, 184, 185–6
Royal Historical Society 113, 174
Royal Institution of South Wales 99, 180

St David's Day 35, 70, 89–90, 134, 188
Sansom, Robert and Arthur 167
Savory, Hubert N. 119, 168
scholarship examination 26, 27–8
Singleton Abbey, Swansea 74, 76, 77
sixth form study 36–7
Smale, George 79
Smith, David 162–3
Smith, Peter 123
South Wales Coalfield Project 162–6
South Wales Miners' Library 163
Spalding, Keith 130
Spaniards in Dowlais 10
sports 14
Stead, Peter 163
Steel, Robert W. 164–5
Stiwdio B 137

students 178
Students' Representative Council
(Swansea) 84
Studies in Welsh History 168
Swansea 74, 76, 77, 78, 84, 88, 99,
113, 136, 160, 175, 190, 191,
197, 198
Maes-yr-haf, Swansea 84
Senior Common Rooms 85, 96,
176
Staff Club 97–8
University College of 73, 74,
76–7, 79, 80–3, 85, 86, 91–7,
107–10, 117, 119, 129, 147,
152, 156, 162–4, 172–4, 176,
181, 183, 187, 190, 194, 197–8
Swansea: An Illustrated History
190–1

teachers, teaching 20–1, 63, 69, 83,
111
university teaching 53, 83
television 136, 138
Thatcher, Margaret, Lady 123, 150
The War Game 141–2
Thomas, Dylan 84, 128
Thomas, George, Viscount
Tonypandy 139
Thomas, J. D. Hugh 96 104
Thomas, Sir John Meurig 86
Thomas, Margaret 64–5, 69
Thomas, P. M. ('Ginge') 114–15
Thomas, W. Ceinfryn 11
Thomas, William D. 78–9, 97
Thomas, W. S. Kenneth 96, 179
Traherne, Sir Cennydd 118–19
travelling scholarships 52–3
Treharne, Reginald F. 54, 59, 65,
71, 73, 111
Tudor, Henry (King Henry VII)
181, 188

unemployment 6
University College, London 49,
58, 106, 114
University of Wales 110–12, 113,
165

University of Wales Press 89–90,
91, 115–16, 166, 170–1, 173,
176, 188, 191–4
Urdd Gobaith Cymru 35–6
Uren, Arthur 127
Urquhart, Donald 154

Vane, Kyra 131
Vaynor 5, 13, 19

Wales 84, 89–90, 95, 106, 124–6,
132, 135, 159, 171–2
Wales and the Reformation 190,
191–4
Walker, David G. 93, 164
Walker, Margaret 93
Walters, Havard 33, 35–6, 38
Watcyn Wyn (Watkin Hezekiah
Williams) 160
Watkins, John Oliver 127–9
Watkins, William J. 67–8
Watson, Steven 153, 172
Welsh Bible 182
Welsh, Welsh-speaking 3, 9–10,
19, 20–1, 26, 35, 38, 48–9, 50,
67–8, 70, 78, 90, 99, 113, 124–
5, 129, 136, 138, 172, 188, 198
Welsh chapels 3, 10–11
Welsh and their Religion, The 191
*Welsh Church from Conquest to
Reformation, The* 115–16, 120,
151–2
Welsh history, Welsh historians
59, 62, 83, 89–90, 91, 94,
106–7, 112, 120, 180, 190
Welsh History Review 120, 165
Welsh Language Act (1967),
124–5, 126
Welsh Language Society *see*
Cymdeithas yr Iaith
Gymraeg
Welsh literature 54, 55, 95
Welsh National Opera 129–30
Welsh Society and Nationhood 176
Western Mail 99, 174
Wheldon, Huw 140, 144
Williams, Alun Llywelyn 90

Williams, Ceinwen (mother) 20,
23, 25, 63, 71, 109, 147, 196
Williams, Dafydd Jones 124
Williams, Daniel (father) 25,
29–30, 63, 71, 108–9, 147, 176,
196
Williams, David 89, 91–2, 95, 111,
116, 119
Williams, Eleri (granddaughter)
176, 199
Williams, Glanmor
activities after official retirement 177–94
on Advisory Council of Public
Record Office 155–7
birth of children 102–3
on Board of British Library
149–55
on Board of Celtic Studies 90–3
chair interviews in Bangor and
Swansea 107–10
as chairman of Broadcasting
Council for Wales 132–41
as chairman of Pantyfedwen
Trusts 158–61
as chairman of Royal
Commission on Ancient and
Historic Monuments and
committee member of Cadw
184–6
and devolution 170–2
Dowlais background 1–13,
18–19
early research 71–3, 86–90, 94–5
editor of *Glamorgan County
History* 118–19, 167–70
as editor of History of Wales
series 166–7
elected Fellow of the British
Academy 181
as governor of BBC (London)
141–7
grandparents and parents 23–5
on Historic Buildings Council
(Wales) 120–3
Inquiry into Welsh Language
124–6

interest in local activities
99–102
interviews at Lampeter and
Aberystwyth 172–4
as justice of the peace 126–8
knighthood 194
as lecturer at University
College of Swansea 74–81,
83–5, 93–9
life as an undergraduate 46–53
love of music 128–31
marriage 82
at Pant school 16–22, 25–6
permanent appointment 83–5
as professor in the 1970s 162–6
as professor of history 110–14,
116–17
publication of *Welsh Church*
115–16
on Royal Commission on
Ancient and Historical
Monuments (Wales) 123
sabbatical year 104–7
scholarship examination 25–8
at secondary school 29–36
in sixth form 36–41
as teacher at Merthyr Intermediate ('County') School
63–71
teachers at university 53–5
at University College of Wales
42–6
as vice-president of University
of Wales, Aberystwyth 186–7
war years 55–62
Williams, Gwilym 38
Williams, Gwyn Alfred 12, 112,
119, 169, 171
Williams, Hazel (née Brown)
(daughter-in-law) 176, 199
Williams, Ieuan M. 116, 120
Williams, J. E. Caerwyn 111, 165,
173
Williams, John Gwynn 112, 123
Williams, Jonathan Huw (son)
102–3, 148, 158, 176, 199
Williams, Leyshon 12

Williams (née Davies), Margaret
    Fay (wife) 46, 60, 62, 72–3, 79,
    80, 82, 83, 88, 89, 96, 100,
    102–3, 108, 110, 119, 127, 148,
    168, 173, 182, 192, 199
Williams (later Robertson),
    Margaret Nest (daughter) 92,
    102–3, 142, 158, 176, 199
Williams, Morgan J. 160–1
Williams, Nia (granddaughter)
    176, 199

Williams, Stephen 78, 110
Wilson, Harold, Lord 142, 143,
    151
World War, First (1914–18) 4, 198
World War, Second (1939–45)
    55–6, 60–1, 91, 114, 198
Wright, Esmond 107

Yesterday's Men 142